There and Back...

Breaking the LEJOGLE record.

Published in Great Britain
by Impressions Publishing
Tel: 01487 843311
www.printandpublish.co.uk

The quote from 'Psychovertical' on p. 122 © Andy Kirkpatrick.

This book is a work of non-fiction based on the life, experiences and
recollections of the author. The author has stated to the publishers that,
except in such minor respects not affecting the substantial accuracy of the
work, the contents of this book are true.

First Edition Published in the USA, 2011
Second Edition Published in Great Britain, 2011
Printed and Bound in Great Britain
Impressions Print and Publish

ISBN: 978-1-908374-18-9

Credits.
Pictures: Unless otherwise stated, photographs are courtesy of Mr. Tom
Emery and arranged by Ms. Kenny Cameron.
Cover Design: Courtesy of Ms. Kenny Cameron.
Grateful acknowledgement is made to Mr. Dave Jessep and Mrs. Sharon
Cox for editing these works prior to publication.

Typeset in 10pt Palatino Linotype

Land's End to John o'Groats and Back

Ben Rockett

Ben Rockett was born in unusual circumstances one cold and gloomy day in December, 1986. Announcing his arrival into the world with extreme hip dysplasia, rhesus disease, a double hernia and severe jaundice, he spent the first months of his life in hospital while his parents were extensively told what he would be unable to do. After mastering movement in his hip frame and putting those congenital 'mishaps' behind him, he grew up in the rural setting of middle Somerset where he spent much time imagining his future explorations and disputing 'what he wouldn't be able to do'.

His intention now is very simple. He wants to encourage others to achieve everything that they're capable of.

To find out more about Ben Rockett go to www.rockettrides.com

To my support team.

For everything you've done.

Acknowledgements:

This ride would have been nothing more than another adventure tucked away in my wooden box of ideas had it not been for a great number of people, who, for whatever reason, believed in me and my mad-cap plan. I would like to use this opportunity to thank those people and all the others who were involved throughout every stage of the ride. Primarily I would like to offer thanks to each member of the support team: Alastair Steel, Ben Allen, Chloe Felton, Dan Tudge, Pete Scull, Tom Emery, Tony Solon and Will Collins, for willingly giving up their time and offering their total efforts to help me achieve this record. Without their support, guidance and directions (which were usually correct) I would never have made it there and back. The impact of such a committed and supportive team is almost impossible to convey, but it was an honour to ride for them and I dedicate this book to each of them.

A hearty thank you to Mum and Dad; you've taught me a great deal about adventure, ambition and acceptance. You've taken me a long way since those uncertain early days. Thank you for being different, but also the same and for choosing the right words at the right time. You know far better than I, the meanings of endurance and commitment.

I must not miss this opportunity to thank the sponsors who put blind faith in the idea without truly knowing anything about me. **Andy Shaw** of the Links Risk Advisory met me as just a simple barman with a crazy zest for cycling. He placed complete trust in my enthusiasm alone, so I thank him for daring to support ambition. The world needs more people like him. I can only hope I did him and his company proud. Perhaps my favourite moment with Andy followed the completion of the ride when he met all the team members together for the first time. He said: "If I'd met these crazy people before hand, I'd never have said yes! I've learned so much from this. Thank you."

A tremendous thank you to every member of **The Bicycle Chain** in Somerset who put up with my continual phone calls and visits without ever losing their patience (that I know of) over the twelve months leading up to the start of the ride. In particular, thank you to Paul Kenchington and Richard Bates for all your interest and cycling passion. During my training I was wearing through bikes and parts at an alarming rate and I am sure the team at The Bicycle Chain were jumping my demands ahead of the queue. To their credit, I had no mechanical issues throughout the entire ride! I think that speaks volumes. Thank you, also, to the Bicycle Chain for sorting out our sponsorship from **High 5 Sports Nutrition**.

Thank you to Phil Griffiths of **Frontline Display International**, Bath, for fronting the funds for our motor home. I hope your arm has recovered from all that twisting. Without the company's support we would have attempted to manage with just a transit van, transforming the interior from a workshop, to a treatment room, to a bedroom, to a navigation centre and to a mobile kitchen. How very Heath Robinson.

Exposure Light's slogan is 'own the night' and thanks to their very generous support this is exactly what we were able to do. Their donation of the MAXX-D lamps was enough to keep the road well lit throughout the long, dark nights.

Thank you to Tyron Dawkins of **Oakley** for his continued support throughout and after the ride. I look forward to working closely with Oakley on future events.

Thanks to **Giant Bikes** for their TCR Advanced SL and Trinity Advanced SL bikes that I was allowed to ride in this attempt.

There were many, many times when it seemed that there was too much ahead of me for the ride to ever be finished. Keeping me going were tens of thousands of people who tracked, called, emailed and showed up on the roadside to urge me a little bit further. Many of whom complained when the red dot stopped as I slept! Thank you for the 24 hour encouragement and seeing me back to Land's End.

And a final, over-sized thank you to my housemates Adi Adams and Nic Bliss, for putting up with all the bikes, rollers, wheels, tubes, cables, dirty cloths and various cans of oil strewn throughout the house. Thank you also for accepting my comings and goings at all hours of the day and night, and for your efforts in keeping me awake through the endless night shifts. I owe you!

Cardiac
Risk *in the*
Young
www.c-r-y.org.uk

Every week in the UK at least 12 apparently fit and healthy young (35 and under) people die of undiagnosed heart conditions.

CRY strives to prevent these tragedies through:

(1) Their National Screening Programme

(2) Funding medical research into young sudden cardiac death

(3) Developing the CRY Centre for Inherited Cardiovascular Conditions and Sports Cardiology

(4) Raising awareness of the risk of undetected cardiac conditions in young people

CRY also supports young people diagnosed with life-threatening cardiac conditions through:

(a) The 'myheart Network'

and those affected by young sudden cardiac death by:

(b) Offering a fast-track expert cardiac pathology service through the CRY Centre for Cardiac Pathology

(c) Providing a Bereavement Support Service

(d) Providing information and literature free of charge

For further information· please visit www.c-r-y.org.uk or www.**testmyheart.org**

Land's End to John o'Groats and Back

5 Days 21 Hours 8 Minutes

1 880 miles

"My greatest fear is being bored. We spend every day with ourselves and our thoughts, so why not make something interesting of our lives. Time continues regardless of what we are doing or where we are going; it will not wait around or slow down just because we do. This scares me. Time runs out and it is impossible to save it, delay it or recoup it. We have one chance to make the most of this time and if we miss that chance then it is gone forever. I want to wisely use every second I'm given and in doing so, encourage others to do the same with theirs. So in reading this, I thank you for taking your time to read a little about how I've used my time and hope that you will find ways to fulfil your own and enrich other's time in turn."

LEJOGLE Facts:

Start / Finish: August 21st @ 09:00hrs / August 27th @ 06:08hrs 2010

Total Time: 5 days 21 hours 8 minutes

Total Miles: 1, 880

Calories Burned: c.105, 000

Weight Lost: 8.1kg

Total Sleep: 210 minutes

Average Distance per Day: 324.1 miles

Elevation gained: 66 956 feet

Punctures: Zero

Foreword: Adi Adams

"Why don't you get someone famous to write this for you?" I asked Ben over a jacket potato and baked beans (the cheapest food we could find on campus), "Some kind of expert perhaps? I mean, what do I know about ultra-endurance events?" He'd just asked me to write the foreword to this book. "You're doing a PhD aren't you?" he replied, "You *are* an expert." In Ben's mind, doing a PhD was as much an effort of endurance as the LEJOGLE feat he had just undertaken. Scraping every last morsel from our plates and washing it down with a cool glass of (free) tap-water, we spoke of the different emotions that he'd been through on the ride, the emotions that we had both encountered along the PhD journey so far, and the qualities needed to complete both; it was a recipe of high self-motivation, commitment, planning, and attention to detail, all rolled up in a bun of anxiety, garnished with a side of self-doubt and a dash of depression. Tasty.

According to Ben, therefore, as an academic sociologist in-training I am expertly qualified to comment in his ride. At first I disagreed; it didn't really make sense for me to do this. We spent the next few minutes pondering the similarities between what for me were the obvious and monumentally different tasks of spending three years writing a 100,000-word dissertation and cycling the best part of 2000 miles in less than six days! But Ben's argument was persuasive and by the end of our lunch I was agreeing that I should indeed write it for him. That's

Ben's unique perspective. He would see things from a different angle to other people and, as was the case with me at that moment, encourage a confidence that it was the most favourable angle. Like the students in that movie "Dead Poet's Society", I felt like Ben was encouraging me to break away from the confines of tradition and to stand on the table to see things in a different way. Thankfully for the other diners I restrained myself, but chatting to Ben that day reminded me of the way he is always trying to see the world differently. The universe really is wider than our view of it, and we are all capable of fine things beyond our immediate grasp. I feel that is the essence of Ben's commitment to this ride, to reach people he can't see and to inspire people he may never meet, and I feel privileged to introduce his story to the universe beyond his own.

In commenting on Ben's journey it's only proper to explain how I know Ben and the kind of friendship we maintain. Ben and I met through what can only be described as an error of administration back in September of 2005. I ended up on the same degree course as Ben with A-Level grades of B,D,D that were well below the entry requirements. After attending a few classes for the degree programme I *thought* I was enrolled on, I soon learned I was mistakenly registered on the same course as Ben, studying Coach Education and Sports Development. So I changed and attended that, kept my mouth shut, and the rest, they say, is history.

Since then, my friendship with Ben has been an interesting one, with ups and downs like any friendship, but ultimately enriching. I would say he knows me better than many people, even some who have known me for a much longer time. I appreciate his relaxed attitude, his calmness, his wit and humour, and his 'counsellor' nature. Yet, for all this, Ben has been a constant source of frustration in the six years I have known him through our undergraduate and postgraduate lives. He can be an enigma, and when you consider someone to be a friend, someone you can open up to, you hope that they can do the same to you – Ben can be hard work in this respect. He rarely reciprocates any emotional "need" from others, and rarely asks for help. I understand that not every person can provide those things; we each need different people to satisfy our different needs in life. Perhaps he is my counsellor, but I do not fulfil that role for him, however much I might wish for that to be the case.

Living together in our first year as PhD students, during Ben's training for LEJOGLE, Ben and I used to joke that we could save money by renting and sharing one room – Ben could sleep in the bed between the hours of 10pm and 4am and I could sleep between 4am and midday. During the daytime we could use it for storing bicycles and assorted oily components, and for studying of course. It was a fine plan, we agreed, and emblematic of our vastly different lives at that time. I was a nocturnal worker and a compulsive, even addicted, day-sleeping graduate student during that year; Ben, however, was rarely beaten to the morning rise by the sun. In one year, Ben must have got himself out of bed before 5am more times than I have done in my entire life.

He goes into more detail about his training and preparation for the ride, and it all seems matter of fact; do this many miles, eat that many calories. However, the reality wasn't so straightforward. Forcing himself to get up and out on the road in horrific weather, or to sit on the 'rollers' (a kind of treadmill for a bicycle which allowed him to rack up the required training miles in his room) for hours and hours, and then refuel with some food, shave his legs, keep up with his PhD work(!) and then get some sleep before doing it all again the next day, for a year, was incredible to experience as an eye-witness. I remember the first time I saw Ben using his rollers – knowing nothing about cycling training techniques this was entirely foreign to me. He made it look easy. And for any of you who have ever tried to do it, you'll know it's not. Needless to say, Ben encouraged me to have a go; I couldn't spin the wheels, and subsequently took a rather ungraceful fall off the rollers sideways. Apparently that was pretty standard behaviour for a first attempt on the rollers. Fortunately there was no damage to his bike and I didn't want to risk causing any and perhaps scuppering his training, so I just left him to it.

One time, I came home to a slow rumbling sound up the stairs from our front door. It was Ben, powering away on his rollers wedged in the small corridor between our kitchen and our living room in the small 3-bed flat we shared with our flatmate, Nicola, above a camping shop in Bath. Ben explained in his characteristic matter-of-fact style: The endurance effort of LEJOGLE would require some serious training; training that would make him pretty tired – understatement of the century. Being on the rollers and falling asleep were not conducive to racking up the training miles, as he'd experienced already. By wedging himself in the corridor, Ben had decided, he could protect himself from falling off the rollers if he was to fall asleep on the bike and thus prevent injuring himself. Should he fall asleep, he'd lean on to the wall but not fall, and touching the wall would wake him up so that he could re-align himself on the rollers and carry on. "Genius" he said, all smug as if he'd cheated nature. "Madness" I said, squeezing past him.

The slow rumble of the rollers was a consistent feature of Ben's training, particularly in poor weather, and echoed through the house intermittently for almost a year. Admittedly, most of the time I was asleep while this was going on, but on many 6am 'toilet trips' I'd walk through the flat to the hypnotic sound of spinning wheels and Bon Jovi or some other outdated motivational rock classics.

As well as the rollers, nutrition was another central part of Ben's training that I witnessed. Many readers may be envious of Ben's crazy need for calories during his training which meant he really could eat anything he wanted, and as much of it as he could stomach. Sometimes he'd have to force more food down even when full, such was his body's need for calories. Now, Ben's kitchen skills are below average, as was his bank account, and these two things make for extreme frugality and extraordinarily boring mealtimes. Upon returning home from a daily cycle, I'd chat with Ben in our kitchen, often with amusement at his culinary creations. A typical five course meal for the 'Rockettman' would begin with a large bowl of cereal. This was the staple 'thinking food', to be consumed while thinking about what to eat next, or more accurately, how to fashion a meal out of the pathetic ingredients in his cupboard. Following the over-sized bowl of cardboardy cereal, it was time for a few slices of warm bread with honey. Then, perhaps a cold tin of sweet corn or baked beans? Why not. A main meal would consist of minced beef, browned-off in the pan, sometimes mixed in with a tin of chopped tomatoes, peppers or onions, but most often not. A couple of satsumas or clementines to wash that down, then, to finish, a box of six jam donuts that he'd picked up in the reduced section at the local supermarket that day. I imagine most people wouldn't find that too appetising for one meal, let alone repeating that a couple of times a day and eating that way for the best part of a year.

Of course, Ben ate well at times, too, and on many occasions relied upon the generosity of others to get his feed – he would often be rushing out to meet up with friends who had invited him over for dinner; unknown to them they'd also invited his locust-like appetite which was sure to devastate their food stores. From a personal point of view, I enjoyed the times when we would cook together – it gave us a chance to catch up on the goings-on of the week, to reflect on what had been, and to contemplate what was ahead. It was also during this time that I perfected my Sticky Toffee Pudding. I was grateful to Ben for his enthusiasm in sampling my many failures before I got it right, and I'm sure Ben was grateful for the calories. I can, therefore, safely say that among the many others, I too contributed to this 'Record Effort'.

Even living with Ben at this time, however, the magnitude of his record attempt never really dawned upon me. Perhaps I was too consumed in my own pursuits; but I really don't think it dawned on Ben either, what he was letting himself in for. Until you walk a mile in someone's shoes, as Ben would often recite to me (a favourite quote of his from Harper Lee's classic *To Kill a Mockingbird*) you'll never truly understand a person. Even with all the miles of training, in Ben's case, unless you've literally attempted to cycle 2000 miles in 6 days then you wouldn't know what to expect. I mean, he had spoken to many experts and endurance cyclists; he was incredibly detailed in his planning, he knew what to expect, when his body would feel good and bad, when his mind might begin to fail him, but the true test was in the 'doing' not in the 'talking about'. And so he did it.

At 11.59am on the 27th August 2010 it was by text message that I heard of Ben's achievement. I still have the message saved to my mobile phone. *"It's a New Weccord!"* The message continued, *"5 days, 21 hours, and 8 minutes."* After almost 6 days spent as "the red dot" on his website's GPS monitor winding his way up the UK and back down again, Ben had found his way back to real life; although I doubt he felt like a real person at that moment. I remember wondering how Ben even had the energy to send that message; I took it as a good sign, a positive statement of his health and state of mind, and felt a huge sense of relief for him, his family, and his friends that he had achieved what he set out to do and had done so with minimal physiological and mental after effects. As it transpired, the cycle had taken its toll on Ben's body and he spent the next few days in hospital; the injuries and "problems" sustained during the cycle are described in rich detail in this book and provide a fantastically eye-opening reflection on the excruciating demands of endurance cycling and on the relationship that Ben has with his own body.

Thankfully, Ben has been recovering well from his adventure, and almost a year from completion, his story is ready to be told. In this foreword, my account of my friendship with Ben and our time spent living together during his training has been rather light-hearted. However, I'm eager not to glorify him too much, for his achievements came at tangible psychological and physical cost. I've tried to capture the seriousness and intensity of Ben's LEJOGLE training, as well as the idiocy and absurdity of it all. Others will laud him for his efforts, and so he deserves it, but they see only the thrilling end result: An astonishing accomplishment and a healthy-again individual making light of his efforts.

So, on this note, I'd like to end my introduction in true Rockett style by leading you into Ben's story with the apt words of Paul Theroux, who hints at the underlying experiences of any journey, that *"Travel is glamorous only in retrospect."*

"The rain was throwing itself down with amazing force. The droplets were bouncing off the road and dancing in front of me, reflecting the lights from the support van behind. My hands were falling apart; the skin so soft from the constant rain. My eyelids were threateningly close together. Attempting to hide my face in the soggy confines of my raincoat served only as a reminder that I wasn't even half way."

"There was nothing left in my body. It was void of all energy and progress South was agonisingly slow. Tears streamed from exhausted eyes but the pain would not go away."

"As the sun was setting, a calmness descended in the valley that carried with it the weight of another night. Having fought to keep me awake, the team were powerless as I repeatedly fell asleep in the saddle."

Tony Solon: "Tiredness was becoming a problem. Additionally he was starting to complain about foot discomfort. I put this down to the fact that it had been lashing rain all evening and that his feet were presumably soaking wet. However I was to learn much later that these were the first symptoms of his broken foot. But like Ben tends to do in his modest manner, he mentioned the discomfort a few times and then proceeded to just absorb the pain within himself, not mentioning it again until near the end of the ride."

"I was down to the last 30 miles. The end was almost in sight but my failing body was barely moving the bike. I still felt so far from the finish."

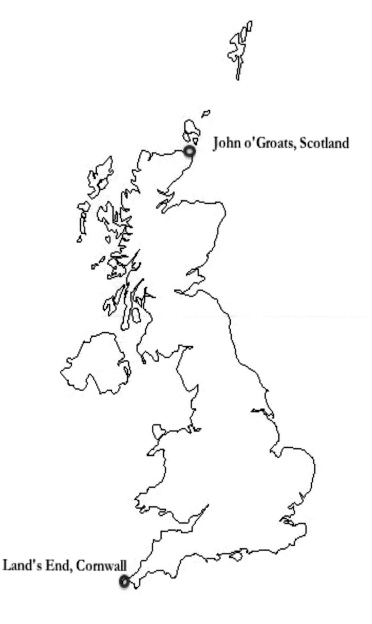

Introduction:

"If we all did the things we are capable of doing, we would astound ourselves."

(T. Edison).

I like to sit in my chair and drift away to an internal world of thoughts and memories, dreams and imagination. That's where I have been writing this. I disappear into a parallel world where anything might be possible and wonder at how I might best bring that world to life. Maps are my greatest inspiration; adventures my greatest motivation. To me they represent ideas above anything else. They show everything that is possible in this world and just how small, yet different our planet is. I think about many of the great people from across this world who have delivered consequential speeches, or those who have completed prodigious acts and marvel at the remarkable difference these people have made. I wonder why those of us who witness these events often fail to recognise their significance as they are occurring.

I sometimes land myself in trouble by verbalising only half my thoughts, placing those around me in a state of confusion or uncertainty. The 'great people' to whom I make reference in that opening paragraph happen to exist, at least in my opinion, all around us. These great people need not be the famous ones we all hear about. Sure, there have been many 'greats' throughout history who have uttered words we all now recognise, or people that we associate with great feats of physical prowess and acts that have led to social change. Yet, while these are significant and deserving of their 'greatness', they are not the events, perhaps, which affect us across the day-to-day system by which we live our lives. Our daily lives are where *we* can make a great difference. The great people are all around us now, and the great people that exist inside ourselves are the people who continually shape that world in which we're living. Actions and words are everywhere; they are no more anyone else's than yours, too.

Throughout the course of this ride, I was keen to share my belief that every one of us is capable of achieving something incredible. There is more inside each of us than we may think. I understand that we won't all be the first to walk on the moon, but the incredible things to which I refer might be teaching someone a new skill, helping a friend or stranger by truly listening, working to make a difference for other people or indeed by bettering ourselves. There is one quote which I would like to borrow to better illustrate my point: "*If we all did the things we are capable of doing, we would astound ourselves*" (Thomas Edison). I truly believe that we all have the potential to astound ourselves. We might do so in very different ways, but I trust we can all astound ourselves - as well as each other. Sometimes we might just need a little extra encouragement, but if we look in the right places we can be sure to find it.

I embarked on this ride to see what I was capable of – physically and mentally. There have been times throughout my relatively short life where I have doubted myself and owing to numerous accidents and misfortunes, where others have doubted me. I was intrigued to understand the boundaries within which I was steering my life. Was I maximising my abilities? Was I making the very most of the time that I'd been given? With this book I will attempt to illustrate what this ride entailed; from the very first spark of an idea, through to what I thought was the finish line at Land's End. The story has been written to give you an idea about the entire process that was involved in breaking the record for it was about much more than simply pedalling.

At the same time as discovering my capabilities, I wanted to complete this ride to show other people how it is possible to commit to something and work for it with utmost determination. There are a vast number of people throughout our world who don't get the chance to live their lives in full. With devastating effect, their death arrives as a complete and utter shock without any warning. The statistics show that this happens to 12 young people each week in the UK alone. They may appear perfectly healthy and lead highly active lives, but undetected problems with their hearts lead to their sudden death. Touched by the caring and dedicated work that they do, I decided to use this ride to raise funds for Cardiac Risk in the Young (CRY) whose mission is to work with cardiologists and family doctors to promote screening and protect the cardiac health of our young.

I was delighted with the support that was shown to CRY through this record attempt. It was an honour to ride the length of Britain twice, knowing that every pedal stroke was raising funds for such a marvellous charity. Thank you to each and every person who so kindly donated – I am, and everyone at CRY, is extremely grateful.

Plenty of people ask about my inspiration for this ride and I can't deny that it's a reasonable question. Part of my inspiration throughout this venture came from one man who is perhaps my cycling idol – Graeme Obree. Why do I think so highly of him? Well I didn't know much about him or his wondrous feats before I was already immersed within my cycling environment, but I learned he also took the 'natural' approach to cycling. There is something about the sport's culture that is obsessed with statistics, training plans / training logs, and energy gels. Perhaps most of that energy is spent 'fitting the bill' for what a cyclist ought to be. At 15 stone and with a bulky frame, I didn't fit into that culture at all. I survived on plain water in my drinks bottle and with bananas, raw jelly or jam sandwiches in my jersey pockets; or heaven forbid, strapped with electrical tape to my frame. I was odd. Neither did I follow a regimented training plan, focused on heart rate zones, wattage or the balance of amino acids and complex carbohydrates in my rigorously shaken powder meals consumed during my tempo or threshold workouts. This wasn't me. I was very simple. I cycled my bike with a balanced diet of natural foodstuffs. Weird, hey? Yes. Quite so.

As well as following the natural diet, I was comforted by Obree's training philosophy. In his own words "the mind is the most important computer there is to use." He calls this the 'feel factor'. He tells people "not to have a training schedule because you can't tell how your body is going to react to each training session. You need the 'feel factor' and sensible diets rather than a meticulously planned training schedule." This guy was up my street. Rather I was up his street – he'd done this well before me.

Obree's story really hit home with me. Many of my 'heroes' in life are actually people I see on a day to day basis, but Obree's mindset is something I admire and aspire toward. Not just for his natural approach, but for three more reasons:

Creative thought.

Self belief.

Razor sharp determination.

Read his story if you want to understand what I mean by these. They are, however, the three features I believe essential to our success in whatever field we direct ourselves. They are the basis of my story and how I achieved the end to end to end record. So please bear in mind: think creatively, believe in yourself and never give up.

1.

"All people dream, but not equally. Those who dream by night in the dusty recesses of their minds wake in the day to find that it was vanity: but the dreamers of the day are dangerous people, for they may act their dream with open eyes, to make it possible."

(T.E. Lawrence).

The idea to cycle from Land's End to John o'Groats and back to Land's End, the end to end to end, or LEJOGLE as it soon became known, came from a fellow student on my undergraduate University course. We had graduated in 2008 and since then we'd taken two very different paths. He was now a teacher, a 'proper job' I kept reminding myself, while I was still playing around with my bike and helping out on the farm.

We met in Bristol for a short reunion with several other friends and watched an unforgettable budget band: Misty's Big Adventure. They were unforgettable for many reasons, but the reason they became lodged in my mind is because I spent most of my time staring at the saxophonist nervously running figures through my mind. The look of concentration and confusion owing to my lack of mathematic prowess I'm sure would have concerned her, but as I sipped slowly at my pineapple juice I became more and more excited by the results I was producing.

Michael Cooper told me about a man from his

home town who was attempting to break an ultra endurance cycling record. Fresh from my 4,000 mile Trans USA ride I was very keen to hear about all adventures, specifically cycling events, so I listened very eagerly. He told me of how this *one man* planned to cycle LEJOGLE in a new record time, breaking the six days and twenty hour record that had stood firm for almost a decade. I'd already cycled JOGLE when I left school, so I was familiar with one direction, but that took me 12 days. I thought six days and twenty hours for both directions sounded ridiculous. I quizzed Coops as much as I could, maybe a little too much, about this man's attempt before sinking into my own world of miles and hours; my own world being a blend of folk songs, dancing hands, pineapple juice and a soon to be over-used calculator.

My very approximate maths told me the record attempt would involve cycling somewhere in the region of 260 miles every twenty-four hours. Two hundred and sixty miles every day for almost a week! You must be joking. At that time the most I'd cycled in one go was one hundred and forty and my rear didn't enjoy that. It did initially seem ludicrous, but perhaps just intimidating. My cycling had come a long way since I had left school. I'd started racing and I was actively trying to become a better cyclist. None of that changed the fact however, that riding almost 2000 miles in six days was a big feat. Yet rather than just give up on the idea, I tried to work out at what speeds such miles would need to be averaged. By this time of the night, the pineapple juices were taking their toll and math sums and dancing were two things I was unable to do. And trying them at the same time was even less successful. I made a note of who Coops said had attempted it and as soon as I woke the next day I started the research. I wanted details and figures; I needed to understand the events of how this record had been set.

It turned out that the challenger from Coops' hometown had already made his attempt, but sadly had to stop at John o'Groats (I would later find that every attempt on the record had been pulled at the half way stage). Having made his way up there in just over three days, Andy Vallance decided that the return journey was not for him, and so the record of six days and twenty hours remained with the man I rapidly came to admire: Bob Brown. After much research I learned that Mr Brown had earned himself the six-day twenty-hour record as yet another notch in his remarkable list of incredible endurance records. The man's CV was enough to frighten anyone; the LEJOGLE record being Mr Brown's comeback following his completion of the Mexican Deca-Ironman race in 1997. I remember sitting in awe as I read of the numerous feats that this man had undertaken, asking myself if I was even being slightly realistic in my thoughts of taking this record. I couldn't yet understand how one person could undergo so much mental fatigue and continue to push themselves toward their goal. How could somebody want something that badly? I wanted a clue as to what motivated him; I was truly in awe of human capabilities.

The more I considered it, the more I felt a draw to be on my bike. If for no other reason than to try and understand the task I was contemplating, I thought that being on the bike would be the best place to think. I worked out the average speed to equal the record, then jumped on the saddle and set out on the roads to see what it felt like. Although this initial pace seemed rather easy, the maths certainly didn't sound easy, and I was very conscious of the duration of the ride: 1900 miles in under a week is not something to be taken lightly. I knew the Tour de France covered around 2000 miles in three weeks so this point played heavily on my mind. I would never be that standard of rider. Yet while this task did not sound easy, it did sound possible. That glimmer of possibility was something that I wasn't prepared to let go of.

Foolishly I hadn't considered the need for sleep or time off the bike and how that would have affected the averages that I had worked out. Of course the average speed would be slower if it also included the rest breaks; the riding would have to be faster than I thought. If I hadn't taken this into consideration, what other glaringly obvious facts was I missing? And how much rest must it require? It was back to the drawing board.

As Adi said, I always attempt to view situations in different ways to the norm. I immediately tried to think about this one differently just to try and make it seem more possible for I was annoyed and intimidated by my lapse in thought. I am a huge fan of Robin Williams: "When you think you know something, you've got to look at it differently." I've learned that a different outlook isn't wrong, it's simply different, and I think that is wonderful. I would have to do something different from all the other attempts if I was going to make a faster return. But what could I do that was so different. Perhaps missing the sleep from my equations was a good idea; it was the answer for how I could save time. But could I avoid sleep for a week and cycle continuously?

I didn't discuss my thoughts any further; with myself or anyone else. I briefly jotted down the general idea and what it would involve before slipping the piece of paper into the wooden box under my bed that holds the rest of my 'would-like-to-do-one-day' ideas. That box is one of the few things I would race back into a burning building to save! Over the next few months I occasionally mulled over those plans and committed it to my long list of things I'd like to attempt. That is, just to make it clear, my way of saying that I wasn't ready for this!

Yet, that 'one day' looked set to come around much sooner than anticipated when I mentioned the event to some of the locals at work. I had since moved back to Bath to study for my PhD and, in order to make ends meet while I was self-funding my research, I was working part time in the Pulteney Arms. I have since learned my lesson that mentioning such ideas to a bunch of connected people soon puts things into action. I was being asked more and more frequently about how my ride plan was developing, when one Friday afternoon, a man ordered his pint and also asked "are you the one who is going to attempt this cycling record for LEJOGLE?"

I can only imagine the look on my face when, for the first time, this idea which had simply been a topic of futuristic dreaming had an air of imminent reality about it. To all intents and purposes, that man was stood there telling me I was going to do it. I didn't feel I had a choice - certainly no choice to avoid it. This was precisely what I needed; a kick-start into getting this underway.

My heart rate soared and my face flushed with the excitement of what I'd just heard. There was something stirring about it. I allowed a slight moment of panic and for my head to wildly spin and speculate. I was trying to do my PhD – what a silly thing to do at the same time. And what is more, I wasn't a distance cyclist. Yet it had been decided that this was going to happen. I was going to attempt to break the record for LEJOGLE (nothing too official, hey?). But at that time it was just October 2009. I confirmed publicly that I was going to attempt it, but I had no idea when. I didn't want to set a date just yet; I'd not really started any preparations! How long does it take to train for something like this anyway? I could delay it for a couple of years, right?

Wrong.

It was starting now. I had a decent amount of

experience with physical training programmes and a sufficient knowledge of the human body to be able to construct my own routines to improve my cycling. I was focused on training at all stages by how my body felt; my training programme was based on being attuned with my body. Being a big believer in self motivation, I decided not to search for a coach, instead taking on the challenge of self coaching and monitoring my own performance over the advancing months. Even when I am coaching other people I encourage them to be proactive in their performance and learning. I was once told by my running coach that his ultimate goal was to put himself out of business by empowering me as the runner with enough knowledge and insight to be the best person to coach me. I have a lot to thank him for, as I've taken that philosophy beyond my running and into everything I do. If we truly teach someone else, then we are handing over knowledge and knowledge seeking tools to others. I don't believe that such a process is ever one-directional either.

I sat and thought extensively about what the ride would demand of me. I say extensively, but even those thoughts were confined to the limited understanding that I had of ultra-distance cycling. I thought about it in the greatest depths I could for many hours, but in the end I reached just one conclusion. The basis of this ride would be extreme endurance – of the body and the mind. I wouldn't be riding as though I was in a short race. I wouldn't even be riding as though I were in a long race. I would be riding in a manner that one rides when they don't plan to stop for a week. I had never attempted that before, so I didn't actually know what that was. But it was what I needed to do. I decided that I would centre my training on time based targets, not distance based. I would charge myself to ride 40-50 hours per week, and the distance I covered was irrelevant. In any case, I was chasing a time target anyway.

In the immediate weeks that followed my decisive commitment to the challenge, I didn't change my training. I just altered my mental approach to cycling. What did the bike now mean to me? What did hills and flat stages mean to me? What would they come to mean? What was the biggest challenge going to be? What would it feel like to live on a bike for that long? I kept my worries and anxiety inside. I didn't want to show any fear at this stage. Not to anyone else anyway.

Over the course of the fortnight that followed I came to terms with the challenge that I *thought* lay before me. I conformed to my usual method of understanding big problems and drew a sort of mind map about how I would gradually extend my ability in the saddle. I use the term mind map, but it looked like I had given all the fear in the world to a mouse and let it run across my page, peeing itself at random points across the paper. At this stage in the preparation I knew I was an average cyclist who had done perhaps a little more than the average person might do on a bike, but none of those events made me a real cyclist. There was still so much I didn't understand about bikes. I sketched my ideas and my plans to learn how to live on a saddle. If nothing in my life had previously, this really shook my world. This was going to be bigger than anything I'd attempted before.

Several more weeks passed and in the run up to Christmas growing numbers of people were talking about the idea of the 'crazy ride'. I'd started increasing my miles further and looking at the road maps to plan in more detail. Sticking to the major roads seemed to provide the shortest distance but I was concerned by the safety of this option. The main purpose of pouring over maps for hours on end was that I felt a sound knowledge of the route would make it easier for me to train, as I could picture sections that I would later face. It was the nearest I could get to 'riding the course' first to familiarise myself with it. I bought numerous books about ultra-distance cycling from the internet to get some more ideas of what would be involved during the event, but also through the lengthy training that I would need in order to get best prepared. I wanted to see where my ideas crossed over with those of people who had already done something similar. Were my plans a million miles from what a plan for this 'should' look like? And if they were, would that matter?

It was during this search that I learned more about the community of ultra-distance cyclists, particularly in relation to the RAAM (Race Across America). These athletes, some year on year, race 3000 miles from West coast to East coast USA, non-stop. The reports I found detailed the stories of riders as they went through hell, reaching breakdowns and physical agony but still finding the resolve to continue cycling. What an event! In perhaps a perverse sort of way, reading about their struggles appealed to me. I wanted to understand what they had been through, but more so I relished that sense of triumph in achieving a set goal in light of such torture.

At the same time as all this harrowing learning and planning for the ride, I was also researching heavily for my PhD. My schedule was entirely filled with reading and cycling. Christmas was all but consumed by books and bikes, and so too was my life. It sounded quite lovely – no other troubles or commitments; just learning and cycling. In many ways it was wonderful and I enjoyed the simplicity of my existence. For that while it was enough to keep me happy and focused. I was balancing the two demands, and although I was missing out on almost all other aspects of life, I was developing quite a social network through the bike. It didn't occur to me how consumed by cycling I'd become until such time as every conversation turned out to be bike related. I now realise how uninteresting this can be for people who do not have such an obsession with cycling.

So now for one of those conversations... I recall sitting in the living room at Will Collins' house; Dan Tudge was there too. We were stuffing some of Tina Collins' Pavlova into our faces, speaking about all sorts of rubbish (as is customary when we're together) as we puffed out the powdery icing sugar. Dan had just returned from the world triathlon champs in Australia and was sporting a fancy gillet that told us so. As a way of trumping Dan's story, I informed them what my intentions were. They looked at each other, Dan questioned my sincerity and Will simply laughed and said "what, you?" Despite their amusement at my idea, I asked them if they'd be keen to help me out as a support crew. I don't know if they really took me seriously, or if they thought this was just another one of 'Ben's ridiculous ideas'. I tried to convince them that I was serious (I forget just how I tried) and I hoped it would slowly dawn on them that this was something I genuinely wanted to undertake.

Please be aware that Will doesn't really take life seriously. He remembers that first meeting along these lines: "I thought he was just coming up with one of our usual brilliant ideas that never actually come to anything. He was sat on my floor chatting about it, which I thought was hilarious. He wanted to put himself through all of that. I guess just to humour him, Dan and I agreed to help him out and drive as support. But then I did not think of it again. I was working in France and would be returning as an unemployed bum, so I thought I had better help out with the ride, and anyway, it would be pretty funny to see him push himself that far!"

Dan's reason for getting involved was somewhat

different. While his first thoughts were logistical, and questioned how we'd get something like this off the ground, he soon became gripped by the physicality of the record. "I was happy just to play with the ideas and discuss them whilst we were riding. In fact some of the most enjoyable planning sessions were conducted after a long training ride, during which we speculated about crazy sponsorship and becoming rich and famous. It eventually dawned on me that Ben would be going through some horrible experiences and I wanted to be involved in helping him through these." Dan would like it known that he didn't really believe this event would lead to any fame and fortune.

Will and Dan are two extraordinarily good friends of mine. Will had spent several years since University working in the Alps, cycling and skiing in accordance with the seasons. He has a very unique personality that shines through every situation and it is almost impossible to spend time with Will without laughing every few moments. We first met at sixth-form where we took a class together, and over the years since, what started simply as company during training has developed into a strong, supportive friendship.

Dan, on the other hand, spends much of his time working within his role in the Royal Air Force. I met him the night before we raced against each other in a triathlon and although we were separated by a few seconds on the day it was immediately after that race that Dan and I started to get to know each other. Dan is completely open and honest. I have a great deal of respect for his ability to speak his mind regardless of the situation and this was a trait I wanted to have in the team. While Will and Dan are very different in just about every way, they share a sense of humour that is perhaps misunderstood from the outside. What many people would, I am sure, consider abuse or mutual bullying, is just their way of removing the seriousness from their lives. They know when to be supportive and sensitive, but they rapidly reintroduce their humour when possible.

Asking Will and Dan to be involved was the first step I had made in constructing some degree of serious team plans. I was still massively underestimating the scale of the project, but I was pleased to have these two on board. I was imagining them sharing the driving of a car while I cycled and they drove from one end to the other (and back of course). They would be able to motivate me with just the right amount of carrot and the right amount of stick, while also being able to help me with mechanics and navigation. What else would I need?!

With this agreement in place, things seemed more definite and I had those two on my case the whole time making sure I wasn't slacking. It was at this point that the 'gears shifted' and I was making a very serious attempt at the record. There could be no half hearted efforts. I had to throw myself into this project with the absolute intention of getting my mind and body to reach and then go beyond any limits they had yet experienced. I would have to push my mental resolve, my emotions, my physical body and my desire to succeed to breaking point. I would break my mind and body into the most worn and useless parts, and then, whilst at my most tired and weak I would learn how to put them back together and continue using them. I perhaps prepared for this in unusual ways. I deliberately didn't feed myself before 100 mile rides or I would deprive myself of sleep the night before a 200 mile ride. I was nervous about how I would react to the demands and so I wanted to trial myself against greater difficulties. I thought it would give me some idea of how I might feel, and at the same time, I wanted to know I could still 'want it' enough to go through it all. Of utmost importance to this ride was my perseverance. At no point would there be room for doubt. I planned for eight months of hard preparation. Eight months of pain, enjoyment, discovery and realisation.

I further increased my weekly mileage on the bike and decided to make training a much more formal activity. I felt that enlisting Will and Dan made it more official and until this point it had all been very casual. I started planning and logging my weekly rides in the diary. I extended my longer ride of five hours and repeated this twice. When my computer read 300 miles per week at an average speed of 18mph I thought I was hitting big miles. I saw 300 miles per week as an intense week of riding compared to anything I had done in training before. Yet I was still completely unfamiliar with what lay ahead. I had been getting by in my old cycling world with one five hour ride per week (c.18mph average) and two 90 minute rides (c.21mph average). I was acutely aware that this wouldn't be enough to get me through seven days of riding. (In fact I had to gradually extend my five hour ride performance to 141 hours.) I didn't even need to carry much food with me on these short rides – sometime I wasn't out for long enough to want water (which is very bad practise). There was so much to learn about the task and my body, and it was a steep learning curve that I found myself clawing at.

Quite clearly with this increase in activity I was eating more and more food. I had been surviving on a small quantity each week, consuming between 2.5 and 3 thousand calories of decent foodstuffs per day. I was leading an active life anyway, running or cycling modest distances each day so I made the most of my appetite. However, once I was increasing my time on the bike I constantly felt hungry. Food would never fill me up, and on the rare occasion that I ate a rich sauce or something super sweet my body would feel full for a few moments. Only a few more moments would pass before I would once again be on the search for food. I started to graze constantly and it became so expensive. I doubled my food bill and was consuming somewhere in the region of 5 000 calories per day - and losing weight. I didn't have time to eat much more food, and given that I am a huge fan of fresh fruit and vegetables, I needed mountains of the stuff to offer me sufficient calories.

The increased volume of cycling caused a phenomenal increase in the amount of sleep I desired. I had been satisfied previously on a small amount of sleep, averaging around six hours per night, but now I needed eight hours just to wake without feeling groggy and heavy eyed. My sleep became much more laboured. I had so many dreams about the ride and often created images of crashes or failing. The ride was playing a significant role in my daily thoughts, but I wasn't prepared for it to take over every aspect of my life; it consumed me at night, too. I had to remember that cycling was something that I enjoyed doing; I had to stop putting pressure on myself.

It was the most simple of tasks to once again find enjoyment for the ride. I just went to new places. I put the maps away, stopped making plans to do other things, and I packed more food in my jersey pockets. I then went wherever I wanted. These urges took me in all directions from Bath and I developed a sound understanding of the area in which I was living. I took in more of the scenery that I was riding through, and I found a mental approach to cycling that I can only describe as 'wanting more'. The more I cycled, the easier it became. Long distances became less daunting, even exciting. I was always wanting more miles, more hours in the saddle, more experiences out on the road and I loved getting lost. I enjoyed messing around with speeds, sprinting when I felt strong, and feeling contented to ride slowly, drinking in the views when I felt tired. I sought out the biggest hills to give me exhilarating descents, flirting with the feeling of losing control. The details of how fast and how far I went meant less and less to me and my diary. I was just concerned with spending as much time as possible on the bike and learning how my body felt.

A dear friend of mine, Sean Cong, shared his concerns with me one evening over dinner that I was viewing my body as a machine; a separate being from my mind. It hadn't occurred to me, but I guess that's exactly what I was doing, and perhaps what I needed to do. I *had* to have that relationship with my body in order to push it beyond its capabilities. I don't want to convey that I was abusing my body in the training for this ride. It was a fine balance between stressing it with increased training, and caring for it so that it would be able to perform. It was a constant battle of dancing between too much and not enough.

At times, the enjoyment of being in the saddle was a real blessing because the weather really was bad that winter. I had been lucky to borrow a set of rollers from Will while he was in France on yet another ski season, and this meant I could still put in my 6-8 hour long rides on the bike, even when the weather was too dangerous to be out on the roads. I won't lie, spending that long on the rollers wasn't the best for reporting on exciting rides, but it did mean I was able to keep my weekly averages up. It also meant, following plenty of practice, that I was able to get through more of my reading.

I placed the rollers in the hallway of my house so I could read my books without too much worry of falling off. The hallway was so narrow that when I leaned too far, my shoulders would simply hit the wall and I'd carry on. When the weather was slightly better but still not great for on the roads, I would place the rollers on the roof of my house and work outside, enjoying the bracing weather, instead of filling my carpet with sweat. I still took every chance I could to get out on the roads and I would ask around the local cycling clubs, from Bath, Bristol and Taunton, on the off chance that there might be some company for a few miles. I was delighted with my physical progress. I was capable of holding a 22mph average for eight hours and still feel strong for interval sets after this. I was getting much stronger and it excited me.

Cycling is a phenomenal way to meet people and company was something I very much sought whilst on the bike. I understood that my circumstances were atypical. Those who hold down a 'proper job' can't take the time to jump on the bike whenever the weather decides it wants to perk up, but that was one luxury I was afforded by doing the PhD. It did mean lots of solitary training sessions though, and this was something I surprisingly grew to enjoy - for a while at least and mainly because I had to. Sadly it most often meant that I was alone on the bike by day, and then alone with my books by night. After five months I was feeling the strain on my social life.

By the time late April / early May had arrived I was regularly hitting 500 miles per week and averaging 21mph. I was becoming too familiar with the roads between Bath and Taunton and I'd fallen into the trap of repeating the rides I was most familiar with so I attempted to find some more new routes to keep my mind from the monotony of what I was doing. I was lucky to have Tony Solon in Bath, the Irish Ox, as he was later named. He tells me that when he first moved to Bath he travelled around by bike with an OS map, learning which roads and routes were connected. When I could tempt him away from his work, I knew it meant a new ride, or at least something a little different. Rides with Tony were full of stimulating and thought provoking conversation which only stopped when we were trying to 'drop' each other; the conversation breaking as we turned our attention to sucking in air. With his help, I would work out when the local rides were setting out from Bath and add them to my already planned sessions, but I would always be envious when the group stopped for a cuppa and cake and I would go on alone. Occasionally somebody would jump on with me and I appreciated this greatly, even if I didn't say much in their company.

It was during this time of riding with Tony and sharing Hartley's jelly that I decided I'd rather like him to be involved in the support team, so I divulged more information to him about what my lunatic intentions were and the reason for my recent obsessive cycling nature. Tony remembers it unfolding much like this: "My personal attachment to this project grew and grew as we discussed the details on many long training rides. But cycling from Land's End to John o'Groats and back again?! Admittedly I hadn't a clue which one was at the bottom and which at the top but that didn't matter, he wanted to cycle it non stop - what a nutter! My kind of nutter though! Where do I sign up for such a mad endeavour? That was my initial thought when Ben told me about his LEJOGLE idea. As a huge fan of all things cycling and not one to miss out on some fun, especially on a bike, I expressed my immediate interest to Ben in knowing more and helping out if I could. After a couple of sit down chats (over my wife's amazing meatloaf) to learn more about this massive project I realised his true determination to turn the project into a reality. I was absolutely sold and gladly offered my services as support when he asked if I would be interested". That was easy! Tony was on board.

Many people express interest in *how* I prepared for the ride. When most people ask me this they are referring to the physical aspects, so those are what I will talk about now. Well, in all honesty I was riding a complete mixture of sessions quite often on a mixed rotation through the week; something a structure focused coach might frown upon! I was riding speed sessions at Castle Combe race circuit (40-50 miles at 24+mph); 50 mile time trial efforts between Bath and Taunton whenever I felt strong enough (25+mph); and endurance rides in all directions, pushing 200 miles on the longest ones (averaging 19mph). I was also filling many hours with extremely slow rides where I would frequently stop to eat, chat to people and sit in fields with great views. These rides were all about helping me recover.

I was also combining all this saddle time with significant stretching and conditioning. I didn't use any weights in training, however, just body weight exercises. At 15 stone I was already on the large side for an endurance cyclist and I was aware that I would need to carry as little spare weight as I could. I deliberately didn't increase my calorie intake to match expenditure when I upped my weekly hours on the bike. I wanted to make my body as lean as possible which meant losing fat and any surplus muscle bulk. I believed I could do everything I needed to by using hill reps, bigger gears and body weight exercises. Despite all my efforts and the six hours a week devoted to hill climbing, I remain to this day a largely useless hill climber!

While my chain and the components may have groaned at this decision to wrestle with inclines, I am pleased that I opted for a minimalist approach. Apart from the bike itself, everything that was going into this ride was natural and was simply an extension of the things one might find in ordinary life. I was just taking them to extremes.

As is all too obvious, cycling and its accompanying factors had taken over my days and I was planning my weeks around the long rides and fitting in the other training sessions. But this was still nothing compared to the later summer months. For the first time my life revolved around training. The washing machine was working over time with the amount of kit that I was putting through, and the food bills were climbing higher and higher. Self-funding my PhD (yes I was still *trying* to do this) meant I had my student eye for life, so I would arrange my long rides to coincide with free meals. Perhaps that's why I ended up in Taunton so often – there's something about the draw of home cooking and knowing there are full cupboards of food. Mid way through one century ride with Simon Williams, a great training partner from Bath, we descended upon the home cupboards and gorged on cakes and biscuits as though we'd never have them again. Thanks parents! We then left and magically the cupboards were refuelled.

Despite my best efforts, the increased level of training meant that I was unable to realistically maintain a healthy balance between training and the PhD. The time I was able to dedicate to study was dwindling and this upset me. I felt I needed to get this ride firmly set so that in my mind there would be an eventual end to this crazy unsustainable existence. After much deliberation and discussion with Will and Dan, we decided to confirm a date for when I would start out from Land's End and so

August 21st was chosen as the most convenient time. In order to get both Will and Dan in the support crew, I had to compromise with a date that fitted around both of their work commitments. Dan was due to be working in Kenya at the start of September, and Will wasn't due back from France until late August. It left a very precise window, but that was all that we had to work with. And I just hoped against hope that it would be ok with Tony. My team of three avid cyclists were keen.

I can't express how much of a relief it was once a start-date had been set. I had been training with a purpose, but without knowing when all the training would find its reason for being. I didn't know how much I could continue to build before I was actually living in the saddle. However, once the date had been set, there was an opportunity for focus and I was able to start thinking about what I had to get done, and most importantly, by what deadlines.

Alastair Steel, the man behind the website **www.rockettrides.com**, had an office in central Bath which soon became the Rockettrides HQ. Into this office flooded maps, phone numbers, brainstorm-boards, very long to-do lists, packets of biscuits (because they're great thinking foods) and lots of excitement and enthusiasm. The excitement and enthusiasm were fantastic, but those attributes alone wouldn't enable the successful completion of the project; we needed a plan. Alastair handed across hours and hours of his time to help with the logistics, planning and ideas for how to make this into a fully functioning reality. He devoted a tremendous amount of energy to the ride, taking on very rich responsibilities completely voluntarily. How do you thank someone for that?

Following lengthy discussions, it dawned on me that this was going to be a much bigger operation than I had considered. I had been very naïve. I was going to need a fairly large support crew, and in turn, a decent support vehicle which was capable of carrying spare bikes, plenty of food, all the people, and the supplies and equipment to keep them and I going for a week. I hadn't really thought about it in this way; I had been too focused on the cycling without enough consideration of the others.

Choosing the full support crew was a mighty challenge for I knew that getting the right people involved was going to be absolutely essential. I needed people with different skills, the right blend of personalities and in many cases, the right experience. This made it a hard task and it took quite some time to decide who to ask. I already had Will, Dan and Tony signed up, but they are mad-cap fans of cycling. How difficult was it going to be convincing other people that they'd also like to be involved? I wracked my brain for who would make excellent candidates. Fortunately (and amazingly) the people I asked required zero persuading! There were the odd few concerns with getting time off work, but they were marvellous and all went out of their way to commit themselves to my challenge. That in itself was a wonderful gesture of kindness, eight times over.

I cornered Pete Scull during a night out in Bath where he was celebrating the end of his time at Uni. I knew a fair bit about Pete, and I knew that he'd have exactly what it took to be cool, calm and collected under all conditions. So I tried to rope him in. Pete recalls: "When Ben first spoke to me about his plans for the summer of 2010, the pieces of information that I managed to retain were 'six days on a bike', just enough hours of sleep to survive and the length of the UK twice! I was both amazed and intrigued about the ride and immediately offered my services to Ben's attempt".

Ben Allen and Tom Emery were equally easy to jump two footed into the situation. I started the phone calls with searching questions about their summer plans, before just diving in with the killer question. Yes and Yes were the replies, giving me a team of six members.

By now, Alastair was eager to lend his services as a support driver. Having someone put themselves forward for a role wasn't something I was expecting so I was surprised but happy to have another confirmed team member. I was, however, concerned that I was lacking any medical knowledge within the team. This would be an essential component to ensuring the survival of the event. I phoned the one person I knew I would be comfortable with and with whom I had complete trust in their ability – Chloe Felton. Chloe and I met back in our sixth form days when we were on the same running team. Chloe had since moved away, trained and qualified as a physiotherapist. If she could be involved then that would be a huge comfort to me. A quick phone call was all it took and I had her on board! Everything looked set and I was supremely confident in the team that was now assembled around me. It was a team that offered every essential skill (minus cooking).

As the calendar turned to June, the planning felt like it was properly underway and I was talking more and more about the ride, with word spreading through the local cycling community. Owing to the support team, and also the support network of friends and training friends that were around me, this pre-ride hype was surprisingly enjoyable. It fuelled the nerves which were mounting but only with the effect of making me cycle more miles.

I think most people considered it a crazy idea and I think the majority were highly sceptical whether it would be possible. Like I said, I'm not exactly built like a cyclist and I certainly hadn't done anything on this scale before. I received a very mixed response ahead of starting. There were those people who were very supportive, frequently enquiring about training and offering their support if it was needed. Equally, there were a number of people who were openly disapproving. A group of cyclists at a track session in June asked me what I thought about "that biggish, long haired bloke who's trying to ride end to end to end" and said "he's not exactly a cyclist to look at". I grinned at how they were asking *my* opinion about this and it confirmed to me that one must never pass judgement of someone they don't know. I responded to them by saying "I hear he's riding huge miles now, so he seems pretty set on it".

I have always respected honesty and I appreciated people who told me I was being silly or that it was an impossible venture for 'someone like me'. These comments made me more determined to attempt it. After all, it couldn't be impossible, because Mr. Brown had already done it! I was prepared to back myself, even in the face of plenty of doubters.

Two people of whom I was keen to get their faith were my parents. It means something when people you respect truly believe that you might be capable of something – it adds clout to the belief that you have inside. I understand that people are motivated in various ways, so it might not be the case for everybody, but I knew I would be motivated by having my parent's faith in me. I had spoken to my Dad about the idea and he expressed his concern about the stress that it would bring, and he asked me if I truly thought I could do it. "Absolutely, yes", I said, hoping those words wouldn't return to slap me in the face. Raised eyebrows and the odd head shake made me doubt his belief in me.

He would ask questions about giving up and at what stage would I get off the bike if I was behind? I was very straight with him and said quite simply that I would complete the ride. I might not break the record but I would certainly get back to Land's End. I had to. If I was so far behind that it would be impossible to beat the record then I would cease putting my body through hell to make it, but I wouldn't fall from the final destination. He seemed doubtful and wanted confirmation that I would 'be sensible', but said he'd support it fully given I seemed pretty set on it. My mother on the other hand said very little when I mentioned it to her. She paused and looked pensive, then said, "that's a long way, Ben".

The questions about quitting sat heavily with me and they were something I wanted to avoid. Yes, I had to be realistic, but I also had to be positive about it, otherwise I wouldn't stand a chance in hell of getting through all the strife. It was going to be tough enough without adding the struggle of beating myself up. Of course I was mindful of the failure – I had to be. I'd never done something like this before, and I was way out of my depth according to past events, but I had to believe in myself.

I used that doubt to motivate some more training. I decided I was going to ride the South West section to 'prove' that I was up to the task; prove it to myself and to my parents. So I did. I set out from Taunton at 0500 one morning and arranged to meet a friend at the end later that afternoon. I figured I could manage that and just about make it back afterwards.

The roads were quiet as I started out and I was passing through the Somerset – Devon border in less than half an hour. I was holding a great average speed to get to Exeter: 23mph. I made it onto the A30 and decided that I would just stay on my drops as much as possible, increasing my pace with the more open road. I remained in the big gears the entire way, straining my hips and my hamstrings at my characteristic slow cadence. I reached Land's End, 161 miles from Taunton just before midday, well ahead of when I had expected. I'd managed to hold a 24.8 mph average for 161 miles through the Westcountry. Remarkably, although I was tired I didn't feel ready to collapse. I was fuelled that day to win my parents faith. My body was comfortable, my mind was relaxed; the dazzling sunshine certainly helped, but all seemed right in the world at that time. There was nothing but the bike and I and it felt wonderful.

That was when I knew I would be able to give this record attempt a good run for its money. To sound cheesier than a croque monsieur, I felt as though the bike and I were really connected. When I told my parents about that trip to the end, I could hear the change and sudden expectation in their voice. Maybe I would be able to attempt it.

As the calendars were turned further and June and July passed through, I was lucky to be riding most days in glorious sunshine. Every day of the week became a long ride compared to all those which I had undertaken previously. My short rides were now six hours (approximately 120 miles) and unless I was completing a speed session, less than six hours felt as though I wasn't doing enough. It really was a pleasure to be out in the saddle while the sun was shining at its best from morning until night. I love being outdoors anyway, but with this weather I was actually spending more time outside than I was inside.

Perhaps you're thinking that my training schedule was relatively laid back with regards to structure? Well I guess it was. I trained according to how my body felt and so I didn't have a regimented plan. I didn't have specific details, rather a vague idea of what I was doing and this philosophy removed a lot of the stress from sticking to a programme. One cannot fall behind a strict schedule if there isn't one in place.

My miles had risen to an average of 750 per week. Monday was still my rest day and I spent it back on the farm, most often thinking about the routes and the company which I had coming up that week. Although my rest day should really have been a complete physical rest, I enjoyed the different labouring of my body. It offered the opportunity to work the muscles in a different way and I enjoyed giving my legs and back a rest from the position of being in the saddle. I looked forward to training and was really enjoying the lifestyle that I had. Maurice and Maureen Bendle would sit and chat with me about the routes which I had taken during the previous week, and against their intricate knowledge of the Somerset / Devon area I learned so many more places which were available to me. Their support was something which really spurred me on throughout the project, not just their generous supply of donuts, and it was a delight and a real comfort to have them see me off from the start line. I owe them an awful lot.

Tuesdays I would generally ride all day, completing about 150 miles before heading up for the Castle Combe track session, hosted by Chippenham Wheelers, where I'd usually accrue, as I said, an additional 40 to 50 miles. Wednesdays I was riding all day, starting around midday and often riding through the night at least until the new morning, sometimes the next afternoon. Thursdays I would seek company to drag me through my tiredness and help me ride between 100 and 150 miles. Friday through to Sunday I would average an absolute minimum of 150 miles each day, still interspersed with hours of stretching and self-massage.

I had seriously altered the way I was riding. I was approaching every session as though my body was unbreakable and I reported my body's functions as though they were mechanical, and separated from my being, just as Sean had highlighted. I discussed my legs as though they were work in progress and as though I had ideas for what they would become. My housemates were regularly commenting on the changes they were noticing in my legs, and on reflection I guess they were right. I was dramatically changing, but I wasn't noticing these physical changes, I was so focused on their working ability and how I could isolate my legs to have better mind control over their performance.

By this time I was also aware that I was burning too many calories compared to my intake. I was constantly feeling tired, and my eyes developed dark bags; the result of too much exercise and too little recovery. I sometimes wondered if I would make the start line – particularly on occasions when the only thing in the world that I wanted to do was sleep. It became a real issue and I found myself drifting into a world of dreams and shut eyes while in tutorials, whilst reading or watching the TV. I was unable to perform an inactive task due to the overwhelming urge to sleep. Trains and buses caused significant troubles for me, and whilst on those, snoring and dribbling caused significant troubles for those around me. I even fell asleep during a brief pause for discussion whilst teaching. During this time the tiredness impacted my personality. I became anxious and uncertain and I lacked the ability to remember simple things and I also started to stammer. I was really suffering. Perhaps I should have been more astute and recognised that I was dangerously close to 'burning out' both on a physical and mental scale. With the right food and the right amount of rest my body was able to repair, and enjoy some time away from the ride. But my mind was a prisoner; it had been entirely consumed by the details and planning of the ride that it could think of nothing else.

I had become well known in my local supermarket

where I would appear morning and night to grab the latest batch of stale donuts. I needed to increase my fat intake and build up some fat stores ahead of the ride. It made sense that fat would be the main energy source throughout the ride, so I started stocking up. I got to know the staff on first name terms, and as the start date grew nearer they would leave the stale donuts aside for me to come and collect them. It was a difficult situation to place myself. I had spent years as a younger person distressed by the fat content of my body and doing everything in my power to remove that distress. I had spent months trying to remove all excess weight from my body and yet here I was now, desperately trying to make myself fatter by consuming ten donuts a day just to sustain what I was doing. Ten stale donuts warmed through and softened by a quick blast in the microwave; something I do not wish to repeat any time soon. The staff in the supermarket must have thought me mad, but I did explain to them why I needed them; although I'm not sure that would have helped my cause.

But that was only the start of my fat binge. I would cut the fat from joints of meat, and lay it between two slices of thickly buttered bread. Then I would add brown sauce or mustard and eat every last drop of it. Part of me thinks I can still feel the fat sitting in my arteries, but I am hoping I have since managed to work off that dreadful diet plan.

I was hugely relieved following the consultation

with my PhD supervisor, Dr Sam Carr, where it was agreed that I would press pause on the research and focus full time on cycling. While this made life much easier, I was always conscious of 'falling behind' in my research. As it happened I enjoyed reading during my more alert times off the saddle, and it provided a good rest from pedalling. The reading also meant I had something to think about while I was out on the bike so I continued the thought processes for my PhD. I didn't have access to a music player, so I made do with my less than adequate singing voice. I would often get fully immersed into a song, singing loudly between my gasping breaths that I would forget when I rolled into a populated area that I was still singing. Particularly the villages of Tetbury and Batheaston must have come to know my terrible singing.

On one of my speed sessions just North of Bath I was repeating the lines of a Bon Jovi song (We weren't born to follow) to act as a distraction against the growing pain in my thighs. I overtook a moped that was screaming along the road and I got a nice buzz from overtaking it on the outside, offering a small nod of the head to the rider. I enjoyed the rider's efforts to make himself more streamlined as he tried to accelerate his steed past me. At 32 mph I pulled across the lane just ahead of him and saw a slight descent in the road. I knew I could pick up some more speed and I set myself the small challenge of beating him to the village of Marshfield about one mile away. My body was screaming at me and my hips were swinging erratically over the saddle. I was red-lining my body. As I opened the gap between myself and the moped rider the words that I was processing in my mind erupted into song and before too many lines I realised there were people around me listening to a dribbling, panting, groaning cyclist blurting out a Bon Jovi rock song. In my sudden realisation I stopped, started grinning to myself and then shared a big show of thumbs as the moped rider passed me, tooting his horn.

I don't know what it is about the longer bike rides, but I firmly believe that they remove the rider's ability to remember more than one line of a song. Over and over I would repeat the same line. I would try and listen to a number of songs before I left the house with the hope that I might be able to remember them during the ride, but there would always be one of those irritating TV adverts or something similar which would creep in. One hundred and fifty miles with 'go compare' stuck in your mind is enough to actually make you like it! I was so stuck with the tune that I created versions of my own (which must be a sign of desperation).

So I was out on the bike for many hours each day. I was also out on the bike for several hours during the night. I had never really done much night riding and I was in need of getting as much experience as possible. And for me, riding through the night was actually really enjoyable. There is an added peace at night that you cannot find during the day. Perhaps it has something to do with the absence of traffic, and the focus of your light, the beam excluding the world around you and all your attention honed in on the area directly in front of the wheel. Whatever the reason, I found it a very pleasurable experience. I would start some rides late in the evening and ride through to morning, and if I felt inspired and moved by the sunrise I'd just keep on going until the following afternoon. I was extending my long rides to 20 hours and this was giving me a good indication of the vast quantities of food that I would need to be consuming.

All this increase perhaps made my task of describing my cycling more challenging. I would pop in for a meeting at University, wearing lycra and dark bags under my eyes whilst wielding a bike through the corridors. When asked about where I'd been, Southampton, Crewe, Oxford, Brecon, Stafford, Gower or Tavistock would return some unbelieving stares. It started to sound like I was living in fantasy land.

I was able to test my endurance of cycling combined with sleep deprivation by competing in a couple of 24 hour races. I competed in the RIDE24, then cycled an 800 mile week, and then competed in the Crudwell24 the following weekend with the Blazing Saddles road cycling club. Needless to say I was pretty tired and useless on the farm that following Monday, but it was perfect experience for what lay ahead of me. The 24 hours races allowed me to really work on some speed endurance. I would find myself chasing down other riders as the laps went by and used the monotony of the environment to really focus my thoughts and feelings on what was happening inside my body.

Resulting from that nine-day period, and from consultation with Nick Willsmer, the man helping with my nutrition plans, I was learning which foods and fluids assisted my cycling and which foods to avoid. I needed something 'normal', something that wasn't syrupy sugar in a small sachet. I opted for chicken wraps, tuna sandwiches, plain water and jam sandwiches. Not the most craze-inducing sports supplements should a shop try to stock them, but certainly everything I needed!

This is one of the topics that many endurance athletes have asked me about since the ride – my decision to consume 'normal' foodstuffs. I guess it is a personal preference, but I struggled to stomach the sugary, sweet energy gels for much more than 12 hours. In fact they would often lead me to vomit on intense hill climbs, or worse, give me an upset stomach and fiery headaches. My body appreciated real food, and I appreciated the need to chew something and not to have to shake it vigorously before gulping it down.

Following the 24 hour races and the hard week of riding between, I felt far better prepared mentally for the challenge that lay ahead. I now had a clearer idea of how I felt when I was exhausted! But I still didn't feel as though I'd experienced enough to know what was going to happen. Short of doing the ride, I didn't know how else to prepare. So I turned inwardly for a cycling focus that would get me through. I tried to produce a psychological tool that I could use to see me through the challenges that lay before me. I needed to create a highly personal process or state of mind through which I would be able to over-ride what I was feeling and what I was doing. I had to teach an automatic pilot.

I decided that my mind would best operate in the absence of a final finish line. I had to stop focusing on the end so I could truly focus on the process that I was involved with. The end was too far away to be helpful; it would only serve to remind me how much there was left to complete, detracting from my input to the present. All feats of endurance will eventually be completed if one continues with the current tasks. I created a comfortable image that I based on one of the roads I'd cycled across the USA. It was a road along which I had no perspective and no concept of time. I could see for almost 400 miles to the Rocky Mountains way off in the distance, but they never appeared to get closer. All I did know was that my legs had one task only – to keep turning the pedals, and if I simply continued to do that I would eventually reach my target. I imagined myself on that road, lost in the feeling of my legs, but able to see for miles and miles around me. I guess it was almost a meditative state where my thoughts seemed to operate very slowly, if I thought at all. It was, in a strange way, a form of relaxation.

This approach enabled me to extend my longest

training rides yet again. I only took on one ride of significant magnitude for I was cognisant of taking on too much before the event itself. I set out to ride 1000 miles continuously. But the beauty of it was that I didn't care how long it would take. I simply had to remain focused on turning the pedals for I knew that eventually I would achieve the set distance of 1000 miles. Nothing else was important (except food and drink); I had nothing else to think about other than keeping the pedals spinning. Often I would ride and stare at my thighs, watching the muscle fibres as they were working so efficiently to maintain my progress. I became obsessed with watching the movement in my knees, and was fascinated at the construction of my leg, which only a few years ago had been subjected to quite serious damage when I was hit by a car. Yet there I was, deeply involved in this task with a leg working for and with me. The human body amazed me; it continues to astound me. It is such a wonderful and complex machine, but we rarely take the time to acknowledge that, or indeed take care of it. Perhaps we all need to risk losing something before we become grateful for what we have.

Although I was creating psychological states to embrace, I was adamant that I didn't want to engage with any form of physical testing. I was becoming aware that my body was changing, but it was changing in a way that I was comfortable with. I didn't want to chart myself against other models of what a body 'should' do or what someone else's body has done in the past. Sports science investigations didn't feature in my mind as something I wanted to do. In hindsight I think such tests would have actually provided extremely rich and interesting data for other people to study. Had we been able to monitor and chart various details of my body throughout the event itself I am sure there could have been some exciting results; I wish I had been more open to the idea from the start, but I am also pleased that I didn't rely on stats and charts to monitor my progression.

I do not believe that a human body can be fully understood as a series of numbers, or indeed deconstructed to just a bunch of descriptive figures. Every aspect of the body works together, and for me the role of the mind is pivotal, which is why at the time I was more concerned for my mind than the physical data that my body was capable of producing. I knew I would need to spend the whole time extensively preparing my mind for what I was going to put it through. The one physical recording that I was interested by, however, was my heart rate. It was rapidly decreasing as the months passed and at the start of the ride in August, my resting heart rate was just 34 beats per minute. Occasionally when I was just drifting off to sleep, I would feel a huge thump in my chest, almost as though it had missed a beat. I learned from the doctor that this was OK!

I eventually discussed my numerous concerns about the ride with as many people as I could, hoping that in sharing my worries they would share some advice. I sought guidance from highly experienced people in the cycling world and learned a great deal from them about the uniqueness of each person's ultra endurance attempt. Many of them suggested I avoid predicting what would happen to me based on other people's experiences. There seemed great consensus in their responses. I could prepare as much as possible, but I wasn't going to fully understand how I would respond to the experience, until such time as I was actually doing it. I now know that they were right on the money.

*****

The last month came and went much faster than all the months previously. I can sense that you want me to get on with the story of the ride! So I will be quick. There seemed a huge number of jobs to do and a huge number of miles that I still wanted to cover. I began noting my training miles on the website since January, and with just a month to go I had accrued 15 thousand miles. I have not detailed every ride through the training, I don't think that is of real interest, but I would like to convey how much of a strain undertaking this training was. Those thousands of miles didn't take into consideration all the other training that was essential throughout; they simply mark the times that I was in the saddle. Between January 1st and August 21st 2010 I had cycled over 18 000 road miles in training. While I was happy with the effort I had put into training and I knew that at this late stage no sessions were going to improve my fitness, I felt a constant need to be on the bike. Oddly enough, it was only when I was on the bike that I could relax.

I found myself getting highly stressed in the last month. I think it was the result of nerves and anxiety, but I could really sense the changes in my personality. I became unsure of many things; I was calling upon the support team to confirm unnecessary details and I was made aware of that stress by those closest to me. I found myself at my happiest when I was on my bike, often alone. I couldn't cope with questions as it made me panic that something wasn't quite right. I struggled with the same conversation over and over, and was grateful to those who wanted to talk about something other than cycling. I guess I was just scared of what lay ahead. I became aware that I was becoming a very intolerant person, and I didn't like that about myself. I remember spending more time at my parent's house, being afforded the luxury of just cycling (on roads where I could lose myself for hours and hours at a time), eating and sleeping. My cycling kit re-appeared clean, the cupboards filled themselves with food, and all the bits and bobs which I left scattered around the house made their own way back to the right places. It must be something about that house.

The support team was working extremely hard behind the scenes. Their roles were clearly defined, they were happy with what they needed to do and they were a super calming influence. Some of my most relaxed times were cycling through the Somerset lanes with Ben Allen. Ben is possibly the most laid back, placid person I have ever met and spending time with Ben was the best remedy for any nerves. He and I would just cycle through the quiet lanes, taking in the wonderful views from the Quantocks and Blackdown hills. Ben is always full of stories and I enjoyed turning the pedals listening to his news. Ben became one of the crew members whom I turned to at my lowest and weakest times. He provided the care and support that I needed and the humorous motivation that only he and his broad Westcountry accent could get away with.

A sentence which I heard so often during the last couple of weeks was: "it'll all come together in time." With August 21st looming over us, I wasn't sharing their confidence, but I left the team to it. We had ideally wanted a motor home to make the journey more pleasant and practical for both myself and the support crew. I was asking these people to drive continuously from one end of Britain to the other and back – they would of course need plenty of sleep to do this safely. I was able to count the remaining days with my fingers when our vehicle sponsor came forward with the answer to our problems. Frontline Display International, based in Bath, offered to sort the hire of a motor home. I am extremely grateful to them for without that wagon, it would have made life much more difficult out on the road. In just a matter of days I heard

Alastair say "I love it when a plan comes together".

It had been a long time, thousands of miles, and plenty of organisational stress since the planning had began. What started out as a one man and his bike idea had grown into a large project. Lots of people were aware of the attempt and there was lots of interest in how events would unfold. The months had whittled away while the training miles had grown and grown. With a very mixed bag of emotions, the time had come to see what was possible. There was no more talk of the future; the ride was very much upon us and the team were all set to tackle the 1900 mile round trip.

2.

"The only way of finding the limits of the possible is by going beyond them into the impossible."
(Arthur C. Clarke).

Friday, August 20th. I had spent much of the morning sorting through piles of cycling kit, boxes of the spare bike parts provided by the Bicycle Chain and eating the necessary amounts of food to feed my hunger. I had been staying at my parent's house and making the most of the extra space to spread everything out, trying my best to establish if I had everything I'd need. It may seem a little late to be thinking about this, but there were still several hours to go which was plenty of time! My perception of having everything I'd need varied greatly, however, from that of Will's. He describes me as the most under-prepared cyclist, so I went to pick him up early in the morning to run over everything that was being taken. It was not surprising that he had many comments to pass on the amount of kit that I had allocated, so he brought much of his own kit to add to the mountains of lycra and tools.

There were also multiple alterations that I wanted to make to the bikes and that required Will's handy work, so he was kept busy working on the four bikes I was taking, plus his bike and Dan's. I was very fortunate to have the support of 'Giant', the bike manufacturer who provided the Giant TCR Advanced SL and Giant Trinity Advanced SL0 for me to undertake this ride. The other two bikes had been my pride and joy since I was much younger and accompanied me, more as moral support than anything practical or for performance gains. In fact, my first road bike made the 'team' of bikes in the support van and is appropriately named 'Old Faithful'. If any of the other bikes failed I knew I could rely on this one to keep working.

The front of the house was covered end to end with bikes and brought home just how real the event now was. I stood back beside my mother, and we looked at all the bikes that would be making this journey. Each of them had been through something with me, either in training or previous events. Mum and I talked about the 'differences' between each of the bikes, the bits I liked and the purpose of such differences. There was a nervous excitement about the place and we busied ourselves with packing and organising as well as running around after the last minute jobs as we thought of them.

Further North, several members of the team had gathered in Bath, loading the Transit van with the food supplies and generic equipment. Alastair, Pete and Tony then headed to collect the motor home on route to Taunton where we were all scheduled to meet. The original plan was for us to leave Taunton at 16:00 in order to arrive at Land's End for a final early night on the pillow. As with all good plans we happened to be delayed and the vehicles didn't meet in Taunton until much later. Loading the bikes, kit, food, support crew's luggage and ourselves into the Transit and the motor home took far longer than anticipated. It was worth taking the time, however, to ensure everything was in a suitable place, and more importantly, that we all knew where everything was.

As the last few bits were unloaded, re-loaded and then moved around again, we were set to depart for Land's End. Or so we thought! My father, the ever observant man that he is, was checking the tyre pressures on the support vehicles and noticed two nails stuck in the rear driver's-side tyre of the Transit van - just what we didn't need. These were causing a slow puncture, so we sat back with a cup of tea while we tried to work out a solution. From a selfish point of view, I was keen to get to Land's End so that I could sleep, but I knew this was obviously an important problem that we needed to fix. Our first thought was to use the spare wheel in the van and we'd jumped on the case of fitting that wheel but upon inspection of the spare, we found a rusty old nail also embedded in the tread of that tyre. I doubt somewhat, that anything had been properly checked after the last time it was hired out.

I had a slight chuckle to myself at how in over 18000 miles of training, I had only picked up three punctures (not with my Bontrager racelites though), and here, before we'd even driven anywhere, we already had two!

With a buffer of some extra air pressure, it was decided that we would embark on the journey with the slow puncture and get the tyre changed at a later stage. We still had to collect Tom from Exeter on route and by this late hour we were all keen to get to Land's End. Starting this event without a decent rest the night before could be a disaster. With that decision made and the contingency arranged for replacing the tyre in Penzance the following morning, we were ready to go.

And then the next issue arrived. My nerves were already taking a fair battering and they were certainly not ready for what happened next. I received a phone call from Chloe, assuming just to say hello and confirm the arrangements for picking her up, but the phone call turned out quite differently. Very sadly, Chloe had been taken ill and was not in a good way. She was unable to come on the challenge. This knocked my confidence dramatically as I knew I would need her on route. I desperately tried to sound relaxed on the phone for Chloe's sake, but also for mine. I didn't want to allow the internal panic which I could feel surging through me to surface; it wouldn't help anything at all. I scrambled through my phonebook trying to find people I knew from related fields and who might know physiotherapists who were prepared and able to drop everything and come to work on the ride for almost a week. I understood that it was a major request and I had little chance of pinning someone down. Rather than delay our departure to any greater length, we jumped into the vehicles and headed South, with concerns and anxiety spinning around our heads.

Obviously the quality of sleep was far from ideal. Firstly, sleeping in a moving vehicle that sways and bounces considerably is not conducive to a peaceful easy snooze, but also the nerves, excitement and apprehensions were keeping my mind as active as a spring lamb. I was also worried about Chloe and hoping she was going to be ok. We had a very quick stop in Exeter where Tom jumped on board and then continued for Land's End. The unfortunate setbacks prior to departure were evidently affecting everyone. The plan that we'd started with appeared to be breaking before I'd turned a single pedal stroke. Tension was apparent in the tempers that were surfacing, and darkness filled the winding lanes of Southern Cornwall while the fog clung to the road; sighs and uneasy silence deafened the van and motor home. We pulled into a pub's car park just short of Land's End, resigned to the fact that nothing else was available. As quickly as we could, we settled down for a couple hours of quiet time, which was more a small chance to all panic without talking about it.

After a restless time squashed in the bed 07:00 arrived and the vehicles became a hive of activity. The set backs from the day before were pushed aside and the team were busy completing all the necessary final tasks. An idle mind is a devil's workshop, so with the many tasks to keep all of us totally occupied, thoughts moved on to getting the ride started – the rest could be sorted later. Pete set to work fixing everyone with breakfast while Tony and Will sorted the bikes in the van. I clambered into the kit that I was to wear, taking time to stand alone and contemplate what I was embarking on. Nothing became clear to me at that point. I just stood beside the van, warmed only by the nerves that made me shiver with anticipation. Having rubbed away the sleepy eyes with my mitts and a healthy dose of excitement, I set off alone, through the thick fog at Sennen, bound for the start line.

Lots of thoughts were rushing through my head as I cycled that mile to the start. Was I fully prepared for what lay ahead? Had I done enough during the last year to make sure everything came together for the course of the next week? Did the team know what they were doing? Would they be able to carry me through the hard times that would ultimately crop up during the 1900 miles? Were my body and mind going to cope with the strain of what I was about to put them under? Will my body survive the stubbornness of my mind?! Alongside all these thoughts and doubt sat a great deal of arousal that I interpreted as excitement and something positive. Countering the nervous tension I was feeling, there was something peaceful about the fog that I was riding through – there was silence all around me and I was focusing on turning very smooth circles with my pedals, listening to the tyres as they moved over the tarmac. I played a little with my gears, sipped a little at my drink, but my belly was too full of nerves for the drink to sit happily.

I was excited about riding my bike for so many miles and I was moved by the thought of getting on the open road and starting this adventure. I saw the South West as something I could enjoy before I was then able to ride on lesser-known roads. There is something about progress that makes cycling a pleasure. I was paying a lot of attention to the memories I had of cycling JOGLE and across the USA previously, and that sense of completeness when all my attention was directed to the road ahead, and nothing else. The demands of my activity matched my perceived ability and I entered the state known as 'flow'. This is highly rewarding and I was able to internalise this as a strong motivating emotion. I happen to love this feeling. I have fallen for the simplicity and clarity of having no particular destination, no particular route, no constraints, and the freedom of thought that enables an open road to show more of its prizes. Through everyday life I seek that freedom, even if for a momentary release of psychological discomfort. I find it highly relaxing and motivating to think about those open-roads and the journey which I was taking along them. Before me now was a very specific route, but I still had that sense of freedom.

One of my strongest cycling memories is of a road through Utah, where the vast, blood red canyon wall to my left dwarfed me alongside the huge open expanse to my right, carved into incredible patterns and shapes by the work of the river and the weather. I could feel the warmth of the sun on my skin and the wonderful feeling of life being breathed into my body through each of my senses. I could feel the water from my bottle flow through my throat and into my stomach – that water giving me the ability to keep pedalling. This was the image I had in my head as the entrance to Land's End suddenly announced its presence from out of the fog. I had arrived at the start of my biggest challenge yet, unsure of what I could expect. Success and failure were in a mighty fine balance, with hope playing a huge role on the side of success. I was now at Land's End, waiting for the clock to catch me up.

I stood chatting, trying to get to talk to everyone who had so wonderfully made the effort to be at the start to see me off. I was able to get a brief moment to chat with my parents, but I didn't do a very good job of discussing my actual feelings. I was really nervous, but my response to everything seemed to be 'yeah, I'm fine. It'll be ok'. I was perhaps saving myself from acknowledging the fact that I was scared of what lay ahead. My mind was put at ease by there being other people embarking on their own LEJOG rides. At the same time there were people waiting to welcome other travellers into Land's End. There was a real rush of activity at the start line that morning which was a welcome distraction; taking my mind away from the task I was moments away from starting.

The support team turned up with both vehicles

and I knew that was a sign that we were nearly ready. It seemed to cause a stir of activity from those who had gathered and the arrival of the vans really changed the atmosphere. Inquisitive comments changed to well wishing comments and conversations drew to a rapid close. The first few photographs by cameraman Tom were met by the last few words of luck from all those gathered at the start line. As Dan announced the arrival of 09:00 I set off from Land's End with 1900 miles ahead of me.

***

I pushed away from the white pillar that I had been resting against; both my feet already clipped into the pedals, and took the first pedal strokes in the record attempt's journey. I was out the saddle in the first 100 meters, feeling the bike beneath me and smiling at making it to this point. This was the moment for which I had been preparing for so long. I'd spent countless hours in the saddle just to make it to this point and yet despite the many ways I'd actually dreamed it would take place, it was over in a matter of seconds. I was along the driveway and out onto the main road in no time and the metres I was putting between myself and the start line stole the sounds of the supporters as the fog stole any view I had of the places around me. The calm atmosphere brought about by the weather was beneficial for the worries and I soon settled into a relaxed rhythm, turning a comfortable gear, just spinning my legs. I rose from my saddle on the climbs, allowing my legs to power me over the bumps of Southernmost Cornwall and to enjoy the feeling of strength in my legs while I could. I had all my faculties about me and the plan was very clear in my mind.

My mind raced over so much that I cannot possibly recall it all, but many of my thoughts surrounded my training, the team behind me and the effort my parents had made to support me throughout this seemingly crazy idea. While my thoughts raced around in a disorganised fashion, the miles were adding up and I was soon over the first few climbs and down towards Penzance. I was making my approach for the A30 – the road on which I'd trained so much in the weeks leading up to August 21st and the road on which I had suffered many of my worst riding experiences. I was apprehensive to say the least.

One of those bad experiences was during a two-day training ride when I ran out of all food and drink. I was attempting to make it to Land's End where I had arranged to stay with my housemate Nicola's family. I had been making terrible progress from the moment I left my house. I struggled against a strong headwind and terrible rain as I made my way to Exeter and this section of the ride consumed all my energy reserves. By the time I reached Exeter I learned that I was unable to ride on the A30 due to extensive road works, so I made my way across Dartmoor, taking in the punishing climbs to Moretonhampstead. My legs screamed, my back burned, my lungs heaved. My body was not coping with this at all. I guzzled my drink and wolfed my food down, hoping it would get me to Tavistock where I decided I would stop for some food and a rest. I'd barely cycled 50 miles and I had nothing left in the tank. The best place for me would have been my bed.

The warmth from the two pasties that I devoured sat in my belly, but the benefit of their calories didn't reach my legs. I still felt extremely empty, hollow in actual fact, and getting back on the bike felt like the worst decision I could make. But with only three weeks until the ride I had it in my mind that I had to continue. I opted for the road to Callington, and from there I would turn to pick up the A30. I was beyond all navigation skills, so I needed to stick to the A30 for simplicity of navigation. I no longer cared if the rules said I couldn't ride it. I fought with myself to cycle past my grandparent's house and continue riding – an argument with myself that boiled over into actual shouting. The A30 offered no sympathy. The wind and rain continued to batter me, and before long in my exhausted state I fell off my bike opposite a petrol station, which happened to have a Subway. I devoured a foot of tuna mayo baguette and slept for an hour before one of the staff asked me to leave. I think my loud snoring perhaps contributed toward them asking me to leave!

I phoned home pleading for mileages to Land's End and numerous other places on route – I wanted to know how far away I was, but at the same time I couldn't bare to think of Land's End as my only target. I continued on the A30 battling the climbs, and then pedalling hard to make it down the other side against the winds. I hit rock bottom on a climb near Redruth. I pulled off into the layby and collapsed onto the floor, wobbling with the sorry attempt at crying. My body was empty and my emotions were unstable. I wasn't recovering and there was nothing I could do about it. I needed to sleep. Despite the rain and the cold, the floor would have to be an adequate place. Resting my bike against the fence, I carefully selected the most comfortable looking section of the concrete and lay down, resting my helmet on the floor as a pillow.

I awoke to the sound of old voices. Two old voices. I was escorted inside a motor home and was given a large portion of a swiss roll. A dear old couple had stopped and taken me into their motor home for some food and to keep warmer than on the floor outside. I explained to them what I was training for, and they thought, I guess quite rightly, that I was perhaps missing a few sandwiches in my picnic basket. A few sandwiches would have been very welcome, but the warmth of being inside and the sweet taste of the swiss roll were a huge help to my recovery. Such kind acts as this one really make me smile about other people. They helped sort me out and get me back on the bike with enough energy to make it a little further down the road. Anyway – back to the start of the ride…

Making the most of my relative mental stability at

this early stage, I was able to follow the signs and easily work out which turns I needed to take. I was able to judge traffic and corners and 'attacked' each of the turns as though I was in a race. I knew once I was on the A30 it was very simple, but there was one stretch which we had been researching for the last couple of weeks. There were more road works along large sections of the road and the Highways Agency had made the decision that cyclists were not allowed to ride on the road between Camborne and Redruth. Will had spent a few years living in those parts while studying for his degree, so he was confident he could lead me through the diversion and back onto the simplicity of the A30. I was uneasy about taking diversions and I was prepared to take the risk of cycling through the no-cycling section of the road. For the sake of potentially being stopped it was decided that Will would navigate me through the area of the diversion.

The traffic was building through the towns and along the connecting road. Although the cost in time and the extra miles caused by taking the diversion were against what I'd hoped for, being so early in the ride this didn't unduly worry me. It was a good opportunity to chat to the team over the radios and also chat to Will who was riding alongside me. We discussed all manner of things, including the route that lay ahead and how we were feeling. It felt nice to have a good conversation, and as was inevitable with Will, there was a lot of joking and tomfoolery. We made our way through the busy high street of Redruth, the buildings jogging memories of how I'd cycled through two weeks before in that very poor state. The road was heavily blocked with weekend traffic and shoppers jumping out between parked cars, so we carefully picked our way back to the main road. As I was exiting the junction I decided that the oncoming bus had potential to bring a premature end to the ride, and my life, so I quickly headed for the kerb. Sadly the kerb was very slippery and I fell off, landing on the road in front of the bus queue. Without any fuss (or any help or hint of concern from the queuing people) I bounced back on the saddle. I didn't feel I had the right to complain about taking the tumble, given not so long ago, Will took an almighty crash right in the centre of Taunton. Of all the people I could grumble to, Will was not one of them, despite his lack of sympathy for me. He almost looked ashamed to be on a bike beside me and simply said: "I didn't think you were getting off the bike during the first day?"

Indeed I hadn't planned to get off the bike in the first day. It was my intention to ride the first 24 hours unbroken and then get a short amount of sleep and 'comfort break' when required thereafter. However, what actually happened was different from the plan. I was cycling faster than the planned average speed (23 rather than 18mph) and therefore felt I could afford to take a short break to get some food into my system without pedalling at the same time. Fluidity in the plan perhaps helped me when it came to the real event. As much as the rigid plan seemed a sensible idea, I preferred to ride in response to how I was feeling and the progress I was making. The plan, therefore, remained largely tucked away in an envelope only to be compared against the ride report at the very end. Regardless, some sympathy for my crash would have been nice!

Before long we were back on the A30 and headed for Exeter. Will was back in the van and I was alone on the bike with just the chatter over the radio for company. Traffic on the A30 was building rapidly and before long there was a gridlock traffic jam. Although I was powered only by pedals, there was soon a sizeable gap created between myself and the support vehicles. I had some food in my pockets, the mental resolve and the physical ability to access that food, and plenty of fluid in my bottles, so I didn't mind that distance. It was good fun riding up the middle of the two lanes with the cars on either side shielding me from the wind. Following prior experiences, I was conscious of cars that might try and change lane, but soon the lines of traffic were moving to give me more space to ride through the middle. The radio signal became broken and then I was very much alone on the bike, but making good progress well above the average speed that I needed to maintain. I questioned whether I was riding too hard, but figured I wouldn't feel this strong in the saddle for quite some time, and given that I felt comfortable, I decided to maintain the pace where it was – 23mph average.

Some of the larger climbs affected the speed, but I was working hard to keep the bike moving above 20mph where I could. I tried to push bigger gears where possible, but settled for higher cadence when necessary. I have a rather odd cycling style where I fight bigger gears in a less than efficient manner; I'm at my happiest when sat in 53-11. I must learn to spin the pedals rather than fight them.

Right then I had a focus on getting to Bristol and I pictured the Severn Bridge when I was down on my drops, trying to keep the riding as smooth as possible. The A30 was being covered much faster than I had planned. Soon I was seeing signs for Exeter and this filled me with the most wonderful sense of progress. Exeter would mean

I'd ridden far through my first 100 miles and this was something I was keen to see on the computer. I only had to complete another 18 of these distances. One hundred miles already meant I was one-third through my minimum daily target, which meant I had already managed to get some hours and miles 'in the bag'.

The support vehicles had caught me by the time I took the Exeter exit and I received the necessary directions from Dan over the radio. I was heading for Tiverton along the A396. This Exe Valley road is a wonderful route and thankfully the surface was smooth and fast. This was a route that I had cycled many times in training also, so I knew what I was riding and where the hills were which required most effort. Local knowledge you could say. Just having an idea of where the top of the hill will be is enough to help the most weary of climbers continue (if they know it's not too far!).

For me, the best part of riding the roads I knew so well was that I was also able to switch off and think about the ride (only temporarily) on a much bigger scale. I had the mind map and the scales of the roads I was riding, unlike the roads up North where I lacked local knowledge. I could picture the roads up to Bristol and I ran them over and over in my mind. The winding undulations of the Exe Valley eventually took me through to the beautiful village of Bickleigh. Although I grew up relatively close to this area, I only discovered the beauty of Bickleigh when I started cycling longer distances. It suddenly appears from along this rural highway and looks so picturesque in its river side setting. However bad I might have been feeling, passing through there always brought a smile to my face. It is just one of the many rural treasures around the country.

Having exited the Exe Valley at Tiverton and headed out onto the dual carriageway that connects the M5 to North Devon I was starting to fatigue and the undulations were to make my legs pay for the increased workload. The A361 is not flat itself and I was again wrestling with the bike to maintain my pace over each of the long climbs. Fortunately I was able to enjoy the long descents too and these graced me with pleasant regularity. I was rolling towards junction 27 of the M5 which meant I was getting close to home.

I was delighted when I saw friends further up the road ready and waiting to jump out and give me some company. They couldn't have arrived at a better time. I was starting to feel really hungry. I had cycled 160 miles and my body was starting its wind down for the end of what it considered a good ride. This was the 'usual' distance that my body cycled and so in a way I had conditioned it to work in 150 mile stints. I knew this feeling of hunger and weakness would become a regular pattern, so I took onboard an extra meal and some fluids and hoped it would perk me up before long. Jeremy Hulse, a good friend from my college days joined me from Tiverton and would remain until Chepstow. It was wonderful to catch up on his news, because as well as genuinely wanting to hear it, Jem was ideal for taking my mind away from the tiredness that was flooding through and dominating my body. I was also starting to feel the effects of the poor sleep the night before and started berating myself and questioning whether I had set out too fast that morning. I was too early into the ride to suffer my first bonk, but this is what it was starting to feel like.

A bonk, for those of you who are not cyclists, is not a moment of interpersonal pleasure, rather it is the depletion of glycogen from the muscles performing in the set task, i.e. cycling. It is a highly uncomfortable situation where the body feels totally empty, often creating feelings of desperate churning in the stomach, extreme hunger, and when most serious, an intense feeling of weakness, helplessness and concern. Often it is coupled with heavy tiredness and the individual simply feels like falling over and going to sleep. Every movement requires maximal effort and the mind becomes consumed by the search for food and sleep. It feels as though every piece of road is a behemoth mountain climb and as though the slightest puff of wind might blow you over. It is most similar to what runners might call 'hitting the wall'. Cyclists just prefer to use an ambiguous term to spark interest.

For me, a bonk was a regular occurrence throughout training. It was not uncommon for my body to experience this several times within a 24-hour period. I bizarrely enjoyed the violent, uncontrollable shaking of my entire body, the inability to focus my eyes and the total incapacity to stand up. It made me feel as though I was working hard. But I knew it wasn't conducive to effective cycling when trying to break a record and it wasn't pleasant for other people to observe, unless of course, like me, they found it amusing. Food held the answer to these problems.

Jem kept me in a decent rhythm however, which meant the pedals were turning and we were soon clocking up the miles again, despite me feeling rather lousy. He would keep asking me about food and while I recall being a really grumpy arse, it was his questioning about how much food I was consuming that kept my food intake up. I owe him for that! He pointed out many of the posters and signs that were left on the road side, including one from my brother's children, Mowgli and Summer. It was so wonderful to pass their house and see the sign they'd put together. I am proud to report that following my ride, Mowgli has completed several long rides – teaching me that it is very possible to be inspired by a six year old.

Passing through Taunton was a case of mixed emotions for me. Taunton, being my home town, was the main centre for support, but I was shocked by just how many people turned out. Arriving in Taunton also meant that we were able to collect our final member of the support crew – Ben Allen. He had to miss the very start owing to work commitments, but we picked Ben up as soon as we entered the town. Ben is a wonderful friend and seeing him at the side of the road waiting to be collected was something I found very reassuring and encouraging. It was as though the team was more complete upon Ben's arrival. His big grin, clasped hands and friendly cheer were a significant relaxant. Fortunately

I knew the roads through Taunton very well so the support van issued no instructions and just set to work sitting on my tail, trying to keep up through the mounting traffic.

Seeing the highly familiar features of the town where I had grown up made me think about the ride in two ways. First I thought about it on a very small scale – the turns, the pot holes, the lights along these streets which I knew so intimately. Secondly I was thinking on a much larger scale; I located Taunton in my mind's map and imagined the distance that stood before my return to this place. That brought on a sense of awe and leaving Taunton almost felt like a second start to the ride. I was actually leaving my home to head North. The route passed directly outside where my parents live and since departing Land's End, I had been expecting to see them there. I looked for them as I passed, but did not see them. I scanned everywhere that I thought they might be, then everywhere else. But they were nowhere to be found. I still don't know whether this was a positive or negative event, because arriving in Taunton made my body feel like it had completed a long training ride and yet there I was expecting it to continue. Had I have seen my folks by my house I think the desire to rest would have been greater, but in their absence I continued along the A38 not expecting to see them until the return journey. Leaving Taunton brought about a strong sense of relief – I had made it through and was continuing with the rest of the journey. Ahead of me lay roads less familiar and I was soon going to be on them.

Plenty of friends and fellow riders turned out to join me through Taunton. In fact, by the time I had reached Bridgwater I had a large group of people who were out to support; those on two wheels, and those at the roadside also. It was a real lifting experience and I enjoyed taking in the smiles and cheers that all of these people were offering. One cyclist who had intended to join me before Taunton failed to do so until well out past the other side of the town. Lee Constable managed to catch sight of the support van as it had picked its way through the town, but he and the van were now several miles behind me and the others. After a quick conversation with the drivers, he performed his very own time trial, skirting around 30mph the entire way until he'd caught up with us. As he rolled alongside me for a friendly and encouraging chat I barely noticed the effects of this effort on him. It was only when the team shouted down the radio in disbelief to tell me just how fast he had cycled to catch up. That's Lee Constable though – one of the strongest riders in the area.

I was very grateful to all those people who cycled far past their initial intentions. They all gave me 'just a few miles more'. They turned back to face a stiff headwind and were caught in a series of extremely heavy downpours. Thank you to all who lined the route at this stage and for all the efforts that went into the banners and posters. I was overjoyed to see so many staff from the Bicycle Chain stores. I am sure there must have been a drop in sales while they all made it out on their bikes for a good hour!

As we approached Bristol the support team's ability to navigate was put to the test. There had been an unfortunate event on the A4 as someone jumped from the suspension bridge, and as a result the road had been closed, meaning we were unable to follow the planned route. The team devised an alternative route immediately and guided me effectively through the city. Despite their accurate diversion, we had been in Bristol for a very long time and I was glad to finally see the signs for the Severn Bridge. We were starting to lose the day's light very quickly and so the team had pulled into Aust services to unload the Giant TCR-Advanced SL, fully equipped with the Exposure MAXX-D lights, which I was to ride through the night. I was met on the road, just outside the services, by a man who I did not recognise, but who was telling me to follow him into the car park. I was in two minds. I wanted to go over the bridge and questioned acting on my own thoughts, but the man looked friendly and in an odd way, very official. I wonder what he would have been thinking as I stared at him, quite clearly not trusting him. Finally the radio confirmed that I could trust this man, and so I followed the giant on his bike. Andy Stewart turned out to be of monumental assistance getting me through South Wales. It was an honour for me to ride with Andy. He is one of the most passionate and enthusiastic cyclists I have had the pleasure to encounter.

It was a super surprise to see my parents in the services car park. It brought a sense of relief to finally see them, but I knew they must have spent a long time driving in the car since their early start to make it to Land's End. I was aware of lots of whispered conversations, I think enquiring about my state of mind and body, but I was happy to express my physical and mental state. I had trained on much longer rides than this, so I hadn't yet gone beyond what I knew I was capable of. This brief change of bikes saw the support crew jumping to action, and they worked seamlessly to ensure everything was ready as fast as possible. They managed this without fault.

I was, however, causing the team some concern already. I was overly obsessed with the speed that I was travelling at and more so with the number of miles I was covering. My tiredness was already leading to mild anxiety and I didn't want to slip behind at any time so I was riding at a faster rate than had been scheduled. But I felt strong, so why not keep going? Once again, the pay back when I was tired was the reason why I shouldn't maintain that pace, but at the time I didn't think anything of it. I concerned the team a lot, for my preoccupation with such details as the speed and distance were hampering my eating. In the 220 miles I'd cycled from Land's End to these services I'd eaten only a handful of cakes, a couple bananas and two chicken wraps. Most of that had been encouraged by Jem's questioning, but I certainly hadn't taken on enough calories and I was reluctant to spend too long putting the food in. It was an act that I would learn to regret further along the route. I have since learned that complete nutrition from the outset is essential. I had been so anal about eating during training, so why was I being silly now? 'You don't eat for the time when you are hungry; you must eat for tomorrow' (Ben Allen, 2010). I'd made my first serious error and the team was all too aware of it.

I hadn't stopped long before I set off from Aust services with a renewed sense of energy. This little stop to change bikes was enough to break the monotony of what I had just done; cycled 220 miles from Land's End. It felt really good to have the South West of England completed and be on the verge of crossing into Wales. This helped me psychologically as it felt like a major step. At the time I didn't want to think about it too much, but I was well ahead of my aggressive targets by the time I arrived at the bridge. I had averaged almost six miles per hour above what I had needed.

3.

"The two most important things I have learned are that you are as powerful and strong as you allow yourself to be, and that the most difficult part of any endeavour is taking the first step; making the first decision."

(R. Davidson).

I had been looking forward to and regularly envisioned the first night ride for I knew it was likely to be the only night ride where I felt reasonably awake. I was guided over the old Severn Bridge by Andy Stewart who then navigated for me until we reached Monmouth. The rain was coming down heavily and there was a tremendous amount of surface water, much like there had been back in Somerset. I was soaked through, but I remember not feeling the cold too badly; I mainly desired food. Andy talked away with the support team and while this was happening I was keen to retreat into my clothing and also into my own mind. I wanted to channel my efforts into maintaining my riding through the night and while I was interested in listening to the jokes I had not the energy to get involved. During the 24 hour races and during my training rides I always noted a performance decrease when my body thought it should really be in a bed, so I tried to avoid getting into too many conversations which might distract me from concentrating on what I needed to do. To exacerbate all those feelings as well, it was like riding through a cold line of power showers at close quarters.

There is something exciting about riding at night, though. When I ride on my own through the dark, it feels very sheltered and peaceful; as I've mentioned, the beam of light ahead is all you can see of the world and the rest of the environment is reduced to shadows and dark outlines. As would become the norm on this journey I also had the lights from the support vehicles. They were tailing me along the A466 using their full beams to light as much of the road as possible. This really made for good progress as the road was as visible as it could have been, but it meant I was always in close range to the roar of an engine.

We hadn't been riding for too long past the bridge, avoiding as best we could but splashing through the numerous puddles, when I cycled straight into a huge pothole. I had obviously been avoiding anything that looked too suspicious, but this patch of water was unavoidable. Sadly for me, the patch of water was filling and hiding a deep, sharp edged hole. The sound produced by my bike and front wheel was amazingly concerning, and the force of entering the pothole had knocked me from my saddle and twisted my handlebars. It also jarred my neck and caused my hands to absorb the weight of my body as they clamped on tight to the bars. I thought I had broken the wheel, picked up a blow out and maybe cracked my fork. The sound of breaking carbon was very worrying so I pulled over immediately and Will was called upon to make the necessary checks and adjustments. After a fair bit of concern on my part, a highly laid back Will Collins handed me the bike and told me to hurry up and get on with some more cycling. "That's not a good enough excuse for a rest" he jested. His confidence in the bike was all I needed and a confidence that I trusted. Dan and Pete shoved some food into me and with those extra calories waiting to be used I set off again, making progress on the A466.

There were a large number of hills along this section making the Wye Valley more challenging than I had remembered. Any hill is more than I would like to remember, particularly if I am climbing it. Previously I had cycled South through the valley, perhaps that being the reason I pictured it so easily. The scenery was once again just wonderful and we were treated to a fully lit Tintern Abbey, which stood out from the darkness in a blaze of glory. The time of night meant there were very few people on the road, and this was the first time since leaving Land's End that we had the road pretty much to ourselves. It made visibility and communication much easier and I felt relieved at not fearing the build up of traffic behind the support vehicles. I could feel my pace slowing on the climbs and I was experiencing a reasonably uncomfortable energy slump.

Since I recovered from the 'bonk' back in Somerset I had been expecting it to return at some stage and I assumed it would happen through the night. Fortunately it wasn't too serious, but it was enough to have an obvious impact on the pace. Tony remembers: "I was a little worried by Ben's expressions of concern at the unexpected inclines on the roads around Monmouth. I too hadn't realised that they 'kicked' so much. But we both knew that darkness can play funny tricks on the mind's perception of inclines/declines. Regardless I was wondering how the hell he was going to sustain the required pace if the first section of hills was causing problems. It was at this point that I realised how often Ben was likely to go through peaks and troughs in his humour and physical condition in a ride of this duration. We took a short break after the first section of hills near Monmouth to regroup. Not long after this we hit flatter roads and were able to settle into a consistent 21mph (17mph on ascents)."

I put most of my problems down to the terrible rain and the temperature. The luxury of the 2010 spring and early summer meant I was accustomed to riding in fair weather, not all this rain. Although I wasn't feeling overly cold, I was suffering from chills in my legs and my calf muscles were unhappy with the situation; my feet felt locked in place and my ankles had lost any sense of mobility. I tried massaging my legs as much I could, but from the saddle I was limited with what I could do whilst trying to maintain the pace. Nevertheless, by the time I had reached Hereford and picked up the A49, I had cycled 260 miles. I was well ahead of the planned schedule so my frustration with the slow speed on the hills was more easily accepted.

Just past Ludlow the team and I met with Clive Middleton. As a RAAM (Race Across America) racer and the 'around Australia' world record holder, Clive was able to give me some really specific support and it was super to ride with someone who knew exactly what I was going through and, more importantly, what I was going to go through for the rest of the ride. I badgered Clive with questions, but that wasn't until I'd received some massage on my quads. I was beginning to get very tight, the result of the cold, wet weather, and me pushing a little too hard since Land's End. My average speed was still 22 mph so I was making strong progress, but the state of my muscles was really concerning me.

The team pulled ahead and found the nearest lay-by where they erected the massage table and had some small bits of food ready for me. My legs were in a pretty bad way and it provided the team with a chance to increase the pain I was experiencing – supposedly for the greater good. Clive's wife, Jude, came to my rescue and set to work with her much more gentle approach while I was covered in blankets and jackets to prevent my body temperature from dropping. We must have created quite a scene in this lay-by: One man lying on a table, flinching and yelping in pain, while multiple people were stood around poking their arms into the mêlée with food, drink, massaging hands, and pieces of paper with messages written on them while two large vans were parked alongside, engines still running as several more people in lycra danced on the spot trying to keep warm. It truly must have been quite a scene because arriving at a great rate of knots with the lights flashing and the siren blaring was a Police car. It was our first encounter with the police, but they bought the story from the support crew that they were actually helping me, not attacking me, and thus the police were happy to leave me on the table buried under all the commotion.

Not a moment too soon I was back in the saddle and was facing a very long section on the A49. Fortunately it was an easy navigational stretch and owing to the straightness of the road, I would soon be through the midlands and into Northern England. As we climbed out of the valley, the A49 became flatter and much more open. At the same time the road became much straighter and the light from the support vehicles enabled visibility much further ahead. The flatter roads coupled with Clive's determination certainly helped me get back into a decent rhythm, pushing an even bigger gear. I was riding along at 27-30 mph and it felt great seeing the computer on the bike reading greater mileage. To hold that pace though I was working extremely hard and was gasping just to get enough air. I would never sustain that speed for any length of time, but that first really flat section seemed to fly by and that feeling was mirrored by the comments which were arriving on the website. The team and I were making positive progress and the surprise from friends and family filled me with greater confidence that we were on track and going over and above what we had set out to do.

Maintaining such a strong pace beside Clive did concern me (and also the waking members of the team). I wondered if I was asking too much of myself, and questioned whether I would ultimately pay the ride-ending price of acting on my feelings of strength once again. I badgered myself about what I was doing, and on several occasions decided to ease back a little, but when riding with others who are keen for some speed, it becomes so much easier to try and inject that extra bit of effort. Perhaps I felt I had something to prove, or that I needed to make some faster progress. Whatever it was, it brought me to ride as though I was in a time trial; a much shorter race than the ride I was currently undertaking! I have since met with Clive and Jude and also Chris Wood, another rider from Black Country Triathletes who had come to ride through the night with me. They said that I actually looked in such a terrible state at Ludlow that they doubted whether I would even make it to John o'Groats.

Passing through the Midlands was the first time I really became aware of the following that the ride was starting to get. We hadn't spent much time publicising the record attempt and we certainly hadn't been plastering it anywhere other than the event website. For that reason I was amazed at how quickly word spread of what was going on. Pete was extremely efficient at passing on the messages as they were arriving, via the website, email or text message. Initially they were written on a white-board and dangled out the window, but very soon they were coming in much too quickly. The radio was used to read the messages to me, but given this was also needed for directions and other communications, the messages soon had to be stopped. I was keen to hear what people were saying, however, so Pete set to work writing them all down and producing them in front of me whenever it was safe or convenient to do so. There were thousands of followers logging on to the website from all around the world and this provided such a boost. To know that so many people were interested in the progress meant I had yet another reason to keep turning the pedals – it also meant I had thousands of reasons not to give up! People were actually following the ride from the corners of the Earth. Across Europe, Russia, Japan, Australia, South Africa, Cameroon, Guatemala, the USA, and Canada. From all over the world people were tracking the red dot that indicated our location.

The red dot actually became a sort of IT metaphor for me and my bike. We were using Google mapping technology linked to a GPS tracker on a mobile phone that updated the map on the website every couple of minutes. It proved extremely popular and was a live, effective way that followers could 'take part' in the journey themselves.

Clive and Chris departed after a couple of hours, heading home to get ready for their day jobs. Their knowledge and their competitive turn of speed brought me to a stage in the country that I considered 'far away' from home. I was reading the names of towns, which to me were a long way away. What shocked me was that I'd reached these places before the sun had even come up. I was approaching the North of England inside my first 24 hours. I expressed this to Tom in the van. He looked at me with wide eyes, smiled, and said "pretty mad isn't it". Yes, I suppose it was.

The closing hours of the night became quite difficult to manage. The team described my mental state as 'starting to slow' and my information processing was taking longer. I was now obsessed with the fear of falling behind schedule. Unlike the long training rides, I now had the potential to 'be behind', and I think this affected me mentally more than I was prepared to admit. It created a strong need to avoid failure. This instigated a reason for anxiety to creep in – I was judging myself against a set target. I didn't want to let myself, or everybody else down by failing.

Pete Scull had just completed his ultra-marathon effort the week before, running 65 miles in just 16 hours, alongside his younger brother and his uncle, and during that event he found the Lucozade energy beans a really big help to his performance. I was starting to feel small twinges in my thighs and my calves were getting tight and sore again. This added to my slumping energy levels, causing me to be harder on myself than perhaps I should have been. I was successfully keeping the worry of physical fatigue away from my conscious thoughts, but the thought of physical injury this early into the ride was not something I wanted to be dealing with. Pete filled Will's pockets with these beans which Will then regularly handed over to me. I can only describe them as morale in Will's hands, for as soon as I was chomping away on them, I felt much more positive, lively and as though I would get through this difficult stage.

I met the awakening of dawn with my arrival through a long series of urban areas. The W's as they were to become known to us…Wigan and Warrington featuring in there somewhere. I was still very much glued to the A49, but I often needed help to find the required turns and exits from the continuous string of roundabouts and traffic lights. We were passing through Warrington, Wigan and Preston in the early hours - the perfect time – and there was nothing else on the roads, so we had the pleasure of relaxed navigation. The sudden abundance of buildings, along with the day's light provided a great contrast to the dark and empty space that I'd just ridden through. I took a few moments to chat with the crew through the windows, but they were keen to get through the urban areas as fast as we could and to that end they kept me riding hard through the cities. I remember feeling a great energy revival at the return of the sunlight; I felt happier in fewer clothes and was energised by the hope that it might be a warmer and drier day. On top of that I could finally see and gain a perspective of my speed.

The support crew have described the significant relationship between the cycles of the sun and my state of mind. Sunset brought about a sense of tiredness and I would battle for a couple of hours, severely decreasing the pace and becoming much more stressed and concerned about injuries, progress and directions. With some food and my personal resignation to the night, I would perk up, both in terms of energy and mood, and offer some form of conversation and interaction. Then the couple of hours pre-dawn I would become extremely tired again and I would fall asleep in the saddle. This caused a great battle for the team to overcome. They knew I had to continue cycling, but they also knew that whilst I was asleep in the saddle, there wasn't much cycling taking place. There was also the added danger that I would fall off.

Their major battle was getting me through to sunrise. We played numerous word games of association, created stories collaboratively, guessed songs as we hummed the tunes, and told many, many inappropriate jokes. I was also posed several tasks to get me thinking about the ride itself; attempting to recall the routes we'd completed and some of the people we'd seen. As I look back now, it seems as though many of these 'games' were simply a way for the team to observe how lucid I was and to judge the degradation of my mental state. Yet, as the sun rose, so too would my morale and my performance. This allowed the team to relax as the struggles with sleep would be gone until the following night. My processing improved, if only a little, and there seemed more hope about the whole undertaking. What a rolling, recurring feeling this was becoming.

Attempting this ride with next to no sleep was by my own design. I had read several accounts of people who had attempted to beat this record since Bob Brown reached six days twenty hours and they all tackled the challenge with allotted periods of sleep each day. Although I had never remained awake and cycled for a week, I figured it *might* be possible and if it was, then that was one sure way of removing time from the record. I wanted to give it a go, and I shaped my training so that I rarely slept between Monday and Friday, and if I did, I kept it to a maximum of a couple hours. I didn't find it easy, and I came to the conclusion that one cannot train the body to exist on zero sleep. But I still wanted to try.

On several occasions during training I would question my desire to ride without sleep, for at my most tired I became weary and highly emotional and I didn't like that at all. I struggled most once I'd found that resting on the aero bars was the most comfortable place to fall asleep, especially with my head so close to my arms. I would most often feel my mind drifting into a sleep and wake myself in time with just a wobble of the bike. On several occasions, however, I woke a little too late and was already half way to the ground. Almost always I fell to the left, landing either on a pavement or a soft verge. One time I veered across the road and woke up only once I was embedded in the hedge. Thankfully I had avoided any oncoming cars. All sleep attacks started in the same way. I would have a thought (about anything) and then explore that in more detail, only the deepest details were considered once I had fallen asleep.

Nonetheless, I set out on the ride with a very aggressive plan as to how I would sleep: basically that plan was to avoid it! While this ultimately afforded me more time in the saddle, and more time moving the bike, it also compounded many of my physical and psychological issues and was the reason for many of my subsequent mental breakdowns. But it was finely monitored by the team and although the sleep caused cyclical issues through each 24 hour period, I still stand by the decision to go with as little sleep as possible.

I remember, when passing through the mass of urbanised streets in the Midlands, how we almost lost Will, and not in a navigational sense. He was riding alongside the van to talk to Pete. I was lagging behind, trying to work out where they were going when I started to watch a slow motion movie right before my eyes. Will had stopped pedalling and was leaning through the window of the van, his arm clamped firmly to the inside of the door for support. I longed to be towed along like that, gaining miles without pedalling, but that of course, would have been cheating. And once I'd watched this incident unfold before my eyes, I was less inclined to get too close to the van! The van was getting nearer and nearer to the kerb. Will was checking, rechecking and checking again the size of the gap as it was steadily decreasing. I watched as he was forced to angle his bike in order to increase the space between him and the van, and then I saw him fully cling on to the side of the van in an act of desperation just as it veered away, providing him a little breathing room. Thankfully he survived without going under the wheels of the transit. What would I have done if my mechanic had to go to hospital?! I questioned whether I should have felt bad for asking him to get me some food and ultimately making him approach the van, but seeing that he hadn't been knocked off and that he was alright, I allowed myself to laugh about it. Nobody was hurt after all, but I didn't think Will appreciated the laughter. He eased off until we were level and I thought he was going to get angry, but he looked at me with a huge grin on his face and said: "Did you see that?! Flipping mental!"

Passing through Lancaster and Kendal filled me with lots of memories from when I made my first end-to-end journey in 2005. I smiled to myself, remembering the events from back then, but also I remembered how relaxed and casual that journey was. Back then I'd had time to enjoy the areas I was passing through. While I was happily thinking of those past rides, I was suddenly directed off the road and into a pub car park at Slyne. There was the massage table set up and Pete was sorting out the meals in the motor home. I learned that I was allowed my first sleep and this was something I cherished. The team noted how badly I had suffered coming out of the first night and decided that it was best to give me a sleep now, rather than risk running my body into the ground completely. I rarely use the word flabbergasted for I feel it describes an extreme form of shock. But at this point I truly was flabbergasted. Upon checking the time I learned it was only 0900. It had only been 24 hours ago that I left Land's End, and I was already 420 miles into the ride: Over 100 miles ahead of where I needed to be at that stage.

A quick massage from the team (yes, it was quite a

team effort), a full belly of warm food and I was out like a light. While Will was busy writing his name on the fence with his urine and while the rest of the team were taking the chance to eat and plan for the road ahead, I awoke in a state of panic. It felt like I had been sleeping for hours and hours and I was concerned the team had forgotten to wake me. I opened my eyes and remember seeing the burly figure of Ben filling the kitchen of the motor home. Why did he look so relaxed? What felt like several hours was in reality, only 20 minutes. My legs felt heavy, but happy for the rest and I immediately wanted to be back on my bike. I recall repeatedly asking for the time and day, obsessed with trying to understand the extent of our progress. I struggled to comprehend being at the end of day one

according to some people (those working in the 24 hours blocks) but 0900 on day two according to others (those using the days of the week). I hadn't been gone long, but I was struggling to process conversation already!

I realised the scale of the ride was a little bit crazy given I had reached this part of England inside the first 24 hours, and I knew how many miles still lay ahead. Between Kendal and Penrith I had the challenge of longer, bigger climbs and this worried me. I have never been the greatest climber owing to my size, but I found these particularly difficult. Most of the team had stopped off in Kendal to collect supplies and to afford themselves a small break away from the stresses of the ride. I had everything I needed in the remaining van, and together we made our way pretty slowly up and over Shap. I was in awe of the scenery, but at that moment in time, I was so focused on trying to keep my pace that I didn't give the scenery the attention it deserved. Tony frequently spoke to me over the radio to keep me company and to offer words of encouragement on what was undoubtedly the hardest climb so far. He also informed me that ahead on the climb, were a couple of cyclists who looked to be climbing at a decent rhythm. I thought if I could catch up with them and sit with their rhythm it might help me get through the discomfort that I was feeling. I was out the saddle, once more wrestling with my bike. But then I was sitting in the saddle, spinning in my easiest gear. Then I'd get frustrated and my knees would get sore, so I'd rise from the saddle again and wrestle with greater resistance. I couldn't find a 'comfortable' position. It was also the first time that the sun decided it wanted to show off its August potential, and tucked tightly inside my full length lycra I began sweating as the sun's light warmed me through.

Somewhere on that climb I developed a 'sensible head' about me and I became concerned about exerting myself too much once again. Perhaps the time trial effort through the Midlands the night before had knocked some sense in to me. I caught the other two cyclists but was already settled into my own happy rhythm. I managed to get a quick conversation with them, and swapped stories of our end to end (to end) rides thus far. Their expressions suggested I was lying and so the disbelief on their faces became mirrored by the disbelief on mine. I enquired with the van for some information, yet again, about time and days and miles. Perhaps I was wrong and I was actually behind. Tony's confirmation that we were indeed well ahead of the schedule, on the approach to 450 miles, gave me a huge amount of relaxed confidence and I remember having a quiet smile to myself. That smile was soon wiped from my face and replaced by a dribbling, groaning grimace when the ascent became even steeper!

Ahead of me I could see yet another cyclist and I wanted to use him to pull me further up the road. I guesstimated that I was 300m behind him, but I wanted to use my old running mind games to pull myself along. I imagined I was attached by a very old piece of elastic which was in danger of snapping if I didn't reduce the tension. With every pedal turn I had to get a little closer to prevent it snapping. I became so focused on drawing this rider in that I forgot to drink and my breathing became highly laboured. Eventually I managed to pick up with this guy who was a local to the area. We had a great chat and soon realised that we were headed for the same destination – John o'Groats. His exquisite local knowledge proved to be a wonderful advantage, and he advised the team on a shorter, more direct entry into Scotland. There was a new road that connected us straight through from Carlisle to Gretna and once he'd pointed this out to us it was plain sailing to the border.

The sun was still shining and the day was offering a fair amount of heat. Owing to this, and the fact that he only rides in decent weather, Dan jumped out and decided to navigate from the saddle, but he was made redundant while Geoff Davis faultlessly whizzed us through Carlisle and out to the main road on the far side, within spitting distance of the Scottish border. After a short while on a new open road, Dan and I were soon through to Gretna and over the border into Scotland. It was a significant moment for the entire team. We were able to mark a considerable step in the journey. Completing the first stage of England in just 30 hours was something I never thought I would be able to manage, but here we were, about to embark on the first half of the Scottish ordeal. We marked the occasion with a celebratory lemon slice and half a banana and without too much adieu, we continued on our way. As we set out, Dan shouted: "It's time for Scotland Rockettman. It's hammer time!

4.

"Fatigue is the best pillow"
(Benjamin Franklin)

Hammer time had to wait for a while. Scotland decided it was time to welcome us properly, so with the exposed A75 to Dumfries followed by the A76 to Kilmarnock I fought a fierce headwind for several hours. My hands were squeezing at the bars, my arms grappling with the bike and my legs turning a very slow cadence as I tried to outmuscle the wind. I could feel the fibres in my quads fatiguing and with every strain of the pedals I could imagine the poor muscle tearing, piece by piece. I wanted to take better care of my legs, but affording them a rest would mean letting up on the effort through the pedals. However much I'd wanted to, I didn't have time to do that. The traffic was starting to build behind me and I was receiving a number of single and double finger messages as well as some loosely gripped wiggling fists as they passed me by. I assumed these hadn't been sent in through the website. This was the first time on the journey that this had happened. Throughout the whole of England I am sure I could tally with just my fingers the amount of troublesome drivers I encountered. Here, in Scotland, I felt they thought I was an English troublemaker. While I do, honestly, understand that it is very frustrating to be held up by slow traffic (I drive too, you know), I didn't feel it was the right situation to keep pulling over. Instead I practiced the art of ignorance (for the most part) and found that it really can be bliss.

I remember being supported most closely by Will, Dan and Ben over this period, mainly for the number of treats that I was receiving from them. Regular fruit pastel deliveries arrived from the van window and this was something I enjoyed – it also gave me a wee chance to have a chat with them. I forget exactly where I decided to remove the earpiece, but I took the radio away to allow me better hearing on the road. I missed the nonsense chatter from the team, save the useless abuse. I felt it was also important to allow the team to pass truthful comment to one another without worrying about softening bad news or omitting thoughts so as not to bring them to my attention. When we were all sharing the same radio signal there was little opportunity for subtle inquisition or questioning from the team. I felt as though they were in a pressured situation to remain positive and encouraging. And anyway, for a change I enjoyed hearing the traffic and the noises of the places I was passing through – it's all part of the experience.

The A76 seemed to continue for a very long time. Perhaps it was the tiredness in my legs, but I remember climbing, very gradually. My legs were still sparring with the heavy winds, not wanting to slip into the smaller gears and spin. As a cyclist I really struggle to spin, spin, spin for I feel like I'm making little progress relative to my pedal turns. Perhaps I am just far too impatient. But it does also hurt my hips. I prefer to pedal very slowly and keep my body perfectly still. The road really wasn't anything too steep, maybe 3% or something, but it was a continual, steady incline joining forces with the wind to reduce my speed sufficiently to make it all too noticeable.

I readily became saddened about my slowing down. Apprehension about progress was starting to worry me more and more and I needed a precise understanding of the miles covered, the times and what day it was (again and again). I started on my day, time and distance interrogations for each of the guys in the vehicles. Repeatedly I would check the mile count, hoping it was climbing faster than I thought. Unless there was an increase of 100 miles or more I felt disappointed. As you can imagine, I felt this most of the time. I worried that I was too slow even immediately after being told I was ahead. Perhaps if I'd asked at intervals longer than twenty minutes I wouldn't have felt so constantly useless! I was aware that I was asking the same question too often when Dan said: "Ben, mate, you're doing fine. We'll tell you if you need to change anything. For now, just concentrate on cycling and we'll let you know when you pass through mile markers. Stop asking for a while. Just enjoy riding your bike".

My shortened progress now made me angry and I was frustrated at being a donkey. I was pissing the team off by always worrying and I didn't want to do that. Tony was always reassuring and with a plain face he'd pass words of encouragement. If I had been days behind, I believe Tony would still have found something positive to tell me. Regardless, I became transfixed on the worry that the team thought I was being useless, despite their telling me that I was doing an ok job. I exclude Will from that, however. When I would moan to Will, or if I expressed my concern about being useless, he wouldn't tame his response at all. He would come out with answers such as "yeah, you're a bit slow at the moment" or "ride faster you fat bastard". Until you know Will, you will think this inappropriate.

After what seemed an eternity, the road became very quiet, much narrower and it passed through fewer and fewer villages. I had been given the target of Kilmarnock and that was where I planned to stop for food and some sleep. Kilmarnock had been my target for months and I pictured it as my first really major milestone in Scotland. We had chosen it as my perspective point – when we thought about how far I should ride in 48 hours, we pictured Kilmarnock as the destination. Fortunately I was going to be there well ahead of schedule. Alastair and Will stayed with me using the transit van while the motor home and the rest of the team drove ahead to cook up some food and find somewhere suitable for the team to have a rest.

I was enjoying a good chat with Will through the window and was positive about reaching Kilmarnock, hopefully before it got dark, and the promise of some warm food almost made it feel like a supported luxury tour. Before I get too carried away with that idea I'd like to stress that it was nothing like a luxury tour, not in any capacity. There were, much to annoyance, some lengthy road works cropping up and while these did not prevent traffic from using the carriageway, the surface was extremely broken and uncomfortable. I had been suffering from pressure sores in the butts of my hands from where I had been leaning on the handlebars with extremely soft hands as caused by the continual rain. The fundamental reason for the troubles was that I hadn't doubled the bar tape prior to starting the ride so I had had very little cushioning through the journey. It was my fault and my laziness at not taking the time to add one more layer of bar tape. There was no other way to look at it. The rough road surface really compounded the troubles and I found myself adjusting my position every few moments, having to squeeze the bars very tightly to alter where my body was absorbing the impact.

There were large blisters developing on my hands, and I was aware that I had very little accurate feeling in my fingers. I was still able to operate the gear shifters, and I could squeeze food and my bottles hard enough to hold on to them, so at that particular time it didn't concern me too much. The uncomfortable road surface did however, start to cause discomfort in my rear end and my knees. The bouncing of my bottom on the saddle and my attempt to soften this with my knees resulted in greater pains and the anxiety that this discomfort brought me initiated a physical bonk. I was pushing Will for exact distances to Kilmarnock, which despite having the map in his hands, he was unable to offer me. This is the same Will Collins who has a geography degree! I am allowing myself to be so naïve as to think that geography is still map reading and place location. Rather than gaining an idea about the remaining distance I instead gained a High5 protein bar – banana flavoured. Will said: "It's this banana bar far, you'll eat it and get there". I laughed at Will for his sense of humour and also for how useless he was. I think he could see in my eyes that I had very little to offer physically, which earned me a rare, but affectionate turn of sympathy. Not that it brought my hot meal any closer to me.

I laboured away for a couple minutes more before Will and Alastair pulled me over for a brief rest owing to the fact that I was barely moving the bike. Alastair informed me that I still had 'a reasonable' distance to make it to Kilmarnock. A 'banana bar far' or a 'reasonable distance'. I just wanted something accurate; was it too much to ask? How far is 'a reasonable' distance?! I would imagine this to be 50 miles; I think I would see that as reasonable, but given my fatigue I was hoping this distance would be smaller. I expressed that I couldn't go much longer without some actual food, but hopped back on the saddle to continue as best I could, hoping I could beat the wobble that had started in my legs. My trembling spread to my face and I could feel my lips wobbling, almost as if I was going to cry. My arms felt hollow, my hands being these alien entities at their ends. My throat felt tight and my eyes bunched together. My belly felt as though it had been removed and soon all I could feel were those bits of me that were in contact with the bike: my feet, my arse and my hands – three parts that were very sore! Everything else seemed so frail that it would blow apart in the wind like a dried dandelion going to seed. Still, I had to get through this and make it through the 'reasonable distance' where I would get that warm food. The next sign indicated Kilmarnock was 24 miles away.

Ordinarily I would see 24 miles and come to terms with that distance. It would usually take just over the hour, but at my current mid-bonk pace, I was looking at almost two hours, if I even made it there. The van radioed ahead to the motor home to notify them of my poor performance. Will uttered such words as "the rocket has crash landed. He is moving slower than an old chipper and is weaker than his erection. He needs some food and to strap on a pair of balls". It was quickly agreed that the motor home would about turn and that we would meet on route. I made it to Cumnock, 15 miles shy of Kilmarnock before we met the van. We utilised an old petrol station, into which Dan piled the truck over a rather high kerb stone. I enjoyed some food, a massage and a brief sleep of ten minutes. I actually recall being in fine spirits and very positive, sharing the team's laugh at how useless my riding pace was. I felt utterly wasteful during this particular bonk, but I knew it was purely physical. I was able to laugh at how pathetic my body was. It was an enjoyable weakness. I hadn't lost my mind and I was looking forward to the trials before me. I felt prepared enough to enjoy them, and I was on a high having spent the last section on the receiving end of Will and Alastair's unique form of encouragement. But there is such a thing as karma. It took a good turn within the motor home...

I couldn't help but notice when entering the motor home, the extremely pungent aroma of urine that had filled the vehicle. I chuckled at the fact that the team were all cooped up inside, inhaling the fumes from the clearly dysfunctional toilet system. The toilet provided significant amusement (for me) on route. We spent much of the first day sitting at very awkward angles to get the jobs done, before realising the pivoting ability of the toilet. We also later learned of the flap that opens the loo to prevent the uncomfortable proximity with one's departed portions. What really caused an issue, however, was the fixing of the collection tank. This was not done correctly, and so what should have been the contents of that tank had wandered off for an adventure of its own, making its way through the motor home, fumigating the atmosphere every time it moved across the floor. It was a really fortunate situation however, that Tom's bag was positioned as such to absorb much of the offending substances. That really is an example of the highest order of taking one for the team. However grim my existence out on the saddle might have been, I could always chuckle at not smelling like a public toilet.

Anyway, I discussed with the team how the road surface and the wind had used a lot of my reserves and that I needed more and more to replace them. My body had reached a point where food was essential, and without some form of nutritional input I would have been unable to go any further. Having this time off the bike at that old petrol station, with the entire team and their unique urinary 'scent' around me, acted like a human refuelling station. There may have been no petrol going into the vehicles, but I was being filled up with morale, support and the team's belief that *we* were going to achieve this ride. Pete capitalised on the moment taking the opportunity to read a lot of the messages to me, adding to the positive feelings and desire to continue. Moments like this are something that I now associate strongly with the ride. Moments when all of us were piled into a van, perched on whatever part of the interior we could fit, learning from each other and doing anything we could to help each other. We shared jokes and stories, filled each other in on the events that had happened, and planned and projected the immediate future. There was always a sense of unity when the whole team was together; it was a pleasure to be there with them.

Before long I was dressed up in some fresh, clean cycling kit and packed back out onto the road. I was still making progress ahead of my schedule, but I was once again concerned with maintaining this. I didn't want my little episode on the approach to Kilmarnock to hamper the efforts, or indeed my opinion about my capability. I was all too aware that my state of mind was going to be essential. Even writing this I am becoming frustrated with recalling how undulating my emotions and abilities were. It must have been such an effort for the team to cater for these extreme and repeated changes in my mood.

After the stop I was really suffering from the sores on my hands; I tried numerous ways of holding my bars, but I was growing increasingly angry at my foolishness at not double taping them – I will now always double tape my bars. Every bump on the road was making them worse and I was aware of how the growing blisters that had appeared were now filling with blood. I tried to burst them, but the lack of fine dexterous skill in my fingers meant I was unable to coordinate this. Instead I tried to burst them by squeezing the bars even harder. My absent grip meant I couldn't, and the result of that effort was seizures in my neck. "Nice work Rockett, a really smart idea".

I continued through Kilmarnock, taking in the town that I had so heavily built up in my mind as my essential milestone. I had mixed feelings about this, but no sooner had I arrived than I shifted my focus to Glasgow.

Although only a short distance away, the night's darkness was arriving and I knew that would mean my urge to go to sleep would again be very strong. I was acutely aware of how my body was already starting to operate poorly. The concerns of staying awake heightened my awareness of the pains and I often dwelled on this which only served to make it feel worse. I felt an intense, but expressionless emotion tattooed on my face as I attempted to come to terms with how I felt. I was entering my second night (or dark time as I later referred to them) since starting and even during training I readily learned that the first night was the easiest by far. Each subsequent night became more and more difficult for me to manage; in front of me now was the start of the second night and I had been riding much harder than I'd attempted in training. Had I concocted a recipe for a disaster?

The undulating road kept me awake and I held a strong pace of around 18mph on the approach to Glasgow with Tony now alongside me. Having consumed plenty of food back in Cumnock I was pleased that life had been breathed back into my muscles and I was starting to feel alive again. My wobbliness had ceased and I could once again put plenty of force through the pedals. The strongest memory I have from this stage was rounding a tight corner of what I can only describe as a wide lane, and seeing all the lights of Glasgow far below us in the distance. The descent was steep, long and full of twists. I was in my element – I love descending, but in my state of fatigue and with the potential disaster of me falling off, the team were clearly a little apprehensive about me fully enjoying the rush of the downhill. I had already shown I was a little unsteady, so reaching speeds above 40mph on a wet surface didn't sit too easily with the team. Needless to say, I felt I'd cycled enough ascents to this point, so enjoying this descent was something I was going to do! That enjoyment didn't prevent my stern telling off though. The road levelled out and I was in a far more urban environment, needing to rely much more heavily on the support team's navigation from the vehicles behind. Faultlessly, as far as I know, we snaked through the outskirts of the city, passing through Paisley and then Erskine.

After plenty of urban riding and with the directions passed through Tony, I made it to the Erskine Bridge. I could place each of the signs and even the lane selection owing to the fact that I'd studied this area significantly on Google street view. I thought back to those images and how the weather changed from screen shot to screen shot. Sadly for me, it didn't change so quickly – I was stuck with the dark of the night and the cold rain. I crossed over the Erskine Bridge with a sense of vigour, feeling once more that I was able to face the highlands of Scotland and make the turn around point at John o'Groats.

Tony and I were still riding at a healthy pace together, hovering around 17mph, chatting and passing the time of night as best we could. We were aware of the traffic on the road, but we were certainly not holding up traffic or causing any troubles. That didn't stop our second encounter with the police, however. Prior to the ride commencing and as a matter of courtesy, Ben Allen had contacted all the constabularies of the counties and regions that we would be passing through. The majority were exceedingly helpful and supportive, with the more local forces even offering to keep an eye out for us while we were 'on their patch'. The Scottish police were less helpful however. They returned Ben's e-mail with a refusal to have any involvement with the ride (not that we were asking them to have an involvement) and an additional warning that we were not to cause any disruptions to the flow of traffic by being too slow: quite a different response to all the other forces. I wondered whether they also gave this warning to caravans, vintage cars and tractors that wished to use Scottish highways. In any case, I was wary of how we would be treated should we encounter a situation.

A police car drove slowly past the transit van and

pulled alongside myself and Tony giving a poker faced stare at what we were doing, before dropping back and aligning themselves next to Dan. I was concerned that we might get pulled over, so I was keen to chat to the police officer in the passenger seat. Having grown up with two police officers as parents I have never considered myself fazed by the presence of the police, particularly in the light of complete innocence. I cycled into the middle of the through-the-window conversation to enquire whether everything was ok. I asked if they wanted me to position myself further ahead of the vehicle to increase my visibility to other road users, to which the officer simply replied "yes". I cycled ahead once more and was quickly passed by the officers who had found their poker faces once more. The team found my interjection quite amusing.

The vigour I was describing upon crossing the river was almost fuelled by that situation and I felt, in some very strange way, more in control having chatted with the officers. However, that vigour would very soon be stamped out by the banks of Loch Lomond. The skies opened, the temperature dropped, the wind picked up and I am certain I would have been drier had I just cycled into the Loch. The road was soon covered in standing water, the aggressive raindrops thundering down into the road and the sound of the vehicle's tyres splashing through the water filled the road with the constant sound of white noise. I found it very stressful and I felt like a tortoise, trying to retract my arms and my head inside the confines of my waterproof jacket. Soon, however, that waterproof jacket was nothing more than another layer; there was so much rain it just soaked me through to the skin. My hands became so soft that the blisters finally perished and to accompany that pain in my hands, the skin on my arse decided that enough was enough.

I mustn't forget that Tony was also out riding with me during this terrible downpour. He was doing his very best to keep me amused and talking the whole time so I didn't become too distressed by the conditions. It was hammering down. Tony and I had ridden fairly recently through Gloucestershire when the clouds unleashed their very best effort. It was raining so hard that it was difficult to keep our eyes open against the onslaught of raindrops in our face. Fortunately it wasn't so cold back then, and we could laugh about the situation; Tony joking that he was feeling a little damp! But here beside Loch Lomond it was heavier rain, and worse, it was much colder. Yet riding beside me, not opting to jump off and get back in the warm and the dry was the Irish Ox, determined to keep me going. Before long, I had had more than enough and I no longer felt like being on the bike. For the first time I was seriously questioning why I was putting myself through all of this. My head dropped and I felt helpless against the onslaught of the rain. I'd have given anything for it to stop. Tony tells me that I turned to him and said "I don't think I want this enough. I might just quit." Although I was feeling extremely lousy, it saddens me that I was so defeatist, and judging by how Tony reported this to me, I think it shocked him, too. The rain was no reason to quit! We still had more than a fighting chance on the record.

Had it not been for Tony's rational thought and explanation, I think this could have been a more serious moment. However Tony just kept me pedalling and made me see that it was a rubbish time to quit. I hadn't even seen the best bits of Scotland and there were plenty more miles that we could cycle together. Giving up at moments like this is the easy option, as Tony told me. He was right. I was just having a momentary loss of enthusiasm and was so fortunate to have had him in the saddle beside me.

The wet weather that I had been so lucky to encounter since Land's End had progressively made my rear end so soft. Marrying a very soft and soggy arse to a hard and unforgiving saddle while that arse is cycling non-stop for so long is a recipe for an adverse result. Sure as saddle sores are saddle sores, my arse was falling apart.

I didn't want to acknowledge this to my conscious self, so I told another part of my brain that it was happening, and that that part of my brain had to learn to deal with it. You may think this is where I first lost my rational functioning, but I found some comfort in dumping these worries onto the 'other person' in my mind; he could deal with it and I would just carry on with the cycling. It actually felt as though someone was skinning my arse, removing the layers of skin one by one every time I turned a pedal. I occasionally felt the pad of my shorts stick to the opened skin, and removing this was made awkward by the lack of control in my hands. I developed an effective technique with the end of the saddle, but I am certain in the following days this became an added factor in the saga of my rear end's continued downfall.

I was in a very unhappy mood when the time came for Tony to jump back in the motor home and get himself rested and dried out, following his epic sub aqua support. I also seized the moment to get in the van and have a brief second out the rain. The feeling of it on the back of my neck and also the constant tapping of it on my helmet was becoming such an irritant. The noise was putting me very on edge. I managed to get some dry clothing on, which was wonderful at the time, but in the immediate minutes after returning back to the monsoon it was really unpleasant as the water barged its way through my many layers. As I was getting dressed I also noticed Will getting into his already soggy cycling gear. I tried to convince him that he didn't need to get out and ride with me and that I could manage on my own, but I was secretly hoping that I could get a few moments to unload my concern onto him. Although I believe I saw a slight glimmer of thought in his eyes, there was no hesitation from Will. He was going to jump out in this weather and join me for several miles. Trying to talk him out of riding his bike is a tough battle – I lost this one, thankfully.

He had been asleep in the 'Crow's nest' (the double bed at the front of the motor home) having spent almost eight hours riding beside me and keeping me entertained further South. Every time he had been out on the bike it had rained. The same was true for Tony, but that's mainly because it had rained constantly. Although I joked about this it became a serious issue because all of their cycling kit was now wet. As I said, despite already being out of dry kit to wear, Will insisted on jumping out beside me and motivating me to continue through this really low period of torrential rain. The team made the decision that because of my weariness and inability to ride in a straight line I had to have some company. Although I wanted to keep my concerns to myself, it was a perfect remedy to unload some of these to Will.

I actually ran out of insults. I said so many nasty, unwarranted, pointless abusive comments to Will, complaining about almost everything, not least the dire weather, until such time as there was a silence. That silence indicated the end of my abusive vocabulary and I was searching for something mean to say, or something about which I could sound very angry. Will saved me the trouble of creating a new abusive word. He turned to me and asked: "When are you going to cheer up, Ben?" It was the perfect response. I smiled at how ridiculous my rant was, and I laughed at how ridiculous the rain was and this whole situation. I also smiled at how wonderful a nature Will had. He was able to put himself out in the worst weather, put up with my anger and abuse, and still encourage, support and be jolly with me in order to keep me going.

I used this time to express some of the emotions inside my head. I opened up and divulged my concerns and fears, and I also shared my pains and problems with him. I feared letting other people down, and the repercussions of not completing the ride. I dreaded the 'I told you so' responses from all those who doubted it and I was immeasurably concerned with the state of my body. Yet, it felt such a relief just to tell someone of the pain that I was feeling. My feet were abysmal; my left foot felt like it was burning and every turn of the pedals made the pain fill my entire lower leg, the sharp pains all meeting in my knee where they appeared to accumulate and intensify, maximising their viciousness in the form of a tearing, twisting pain. I am a very anti-medication person; I don't like to take any medicines if I can really help it, and so I was very reluctant to take anything at all. It was obvious what was causing them! However, I finally failed and took some ibuprofen to try and reduce the dramatically increasing swelling in my knee.

I jumped off briefly, after much complaining and discomfort, to try and establish what the problem was with my foot. I reached the stage where I was sure there must be something visibly wrong with my foot, and I thought, if I can see the problem, I can fix it. Sadly, the troubles were deep inside my foot – problems I would later find out to be fractured metatarsals. The team set to work to try and make it more comfortable, the sogginess of the foot and the terrible skin condition being something they wanted to sort out. I changed my shoes to a dry pair and felt a little more human. Looking back now I laugh at the memory, but Tony and Ben were sprinkling talcum powder onto my feet in an attempt to reduce the discomfort. With the knowledge now that it was fractured makes me smile at the thought of applying talcum powder to help a bone heal. Still, I was grateful for the efforts and the care that they took. Sadly for Will, it didn't help the problem and so my angry and emotional outbursts continued for him. I hope he saw it as a compliment that I felt comfortable enough that I could break down with him!

I get particularly amazed at how the human mind deals with regular events. By that I mean I am amazed at how being overly familiar with something reduces how impressed we are by it. It happens with great foods, great views, great people – once we're highly familiar with something it loses its awe. I think that is a great shame. I think it is important to take stock of the familiar things in life and recognise that we are very lucky to have such wonderous things. My bike is one example. When I first got it, I was amazed with it; how it felt to ride, how it handled on corners, how light it was and how it looked when it was clean. All of these points remained the same every time I cycled it (well, if I cleaned it from the ride before!); although I no longer get excited about it. It is now 'just my bike'. What a shame!

When I was passing through Scotland I was aware that the scenery was truly impressive. Ok, so during the night in the pouring rain I was unable to see it, but it was still a pretty dramatic place to be. I know I was not really on a sightseeing mission, but there is still the opportunity to enjoy the scenery that I was lucky enough to be passing. But I didn't. I pretty much ignored it after the first couple of comments about it being 'lovely' and 'wonderful'. I was being enough of a feather with the bike that I didn't need any more airy-fairy comments to add to it.

After leaving the flanks of Loch Lomond, I cycled over many undulations before taking in a long, steady climb to the top of the Great Glen. The route was up and over Rannoch Moor. Thankfully the rain eased back, and for a brief while, the wind also eased, allowing me to climb in good conditions aside from the darkness of the middle of the night. While the road was empty of other users, we had plenty of company from the ridiculous numbers of red deer. There were hundreds of them all along the road, and I can only imagine there were tremendous amounts more hidden away in the darkness. They kept me amused, particularly those closest to the road who would turn and run as soon as the distance between us and them decreased. I am sure even these creatures looked at our collection of life and thought it insane.

It was a long climb; one which I remember descending five years ago into a very stiff headwind. I wished for that same wind to help me up the climb this time, but I was happy in the rhythm that I was able to keep. I kept saying that there was a huge descent coming up soon – I could remember it accurately from my time before. I cycled for another half an hour or so, steadily climbing when I turned to Will and promised him that the descent would be coming up very soon. Another half hour passed with plenty of climbing still on route. All of a sudden we started heading down a very long, fast and winding descent. I am sure Will was ignoring every comment I was making by this stage, but I did turn to him and point out the fact that I'd remembered it – albeit inaccurately, but there was a descent.

Dan was driving the transit van, and was doing his best to tail us very closely. I enjoyed having Dan close by as he provided a distraction and would help take my mind away from the task at hand. He was driving with Ben and they would regularly pull up alongside just so we could have a chat through the window. One of those chats that just lets you know they're there for you. A few brief words to show they care. Often they would pass food out to me and I would pile it in as quickly as possible, all the while, Dan uttering words of encouragement and offering details about the progress. Dan was never fazed by anything I told him. If I said something was wrong or I had troubles or if I wanted to say something about the team, he listened without judgement and told me the plan of action, making sure he sorted out any issue. Even if I had an issue with him or something he'd done, I could just voice that thought and he would put it right. Dan always had the right words for every occasion.

His driving was also responsible for preventing several spoils from the saddle. I arrived in Fort William with Will still riding alongside me (part of his 11 hour stint), only now he was beside me for a very different reason than just to keep me company. As the morning was arriving I began to feel the effects of another missed sleep. I expressed to Will that I was feeling really tired and that it felt like I would fall asleep at any point. I was asking for a short sleep break but the team was saying I had to push on. I was unsure if I would be able to manage much further with my eyes open, but I knew I was going to be pressured into staying on the bike. I wasn't even half way through the ride so there was no chance that I could afford any added breaks. But my eyelids were getting closer and closer together. The sound of the van was getting further and further away as my brain entered micro-sleeps, and the thoughts that were running through my head were becoming more and more detailed. I dreamed of when I was scuba diving in Egypt, my dive partner Jess Todd and I turning to follow an octopus along the coral. It seemed so real; I felt I was below the surface of the red sea and I could feel the water against my face and see all the fish so clearly that I felt I could reach out and touch them.

I woke with a start to the sound of Will's voice while he was slapping me. I had fallen asleep on the bike; I didn't know for how long. I remembered I was on a bike and just started pedalling again trying to recall any conversation that had been happening between Will and I but I wasn't sure what I was actually riding for. Will told me that I was close to Fort William and that once I was there I could have a short rest. I could feel my head dropping, my eyelids getting closer together and soon enough I was once more asleep in the saddle. Dan sounded the horn from the van and this again woke me with a startle, my legs instantly back to their job of pedalling. I looked at Will who looked slightly concerned. Only slightly concerned I might add. Apparently he was turning to the van, pointing and laughing at how ridiculous I looked sleeping in the saddle. On a positive note, however, he had positioned himself right next to me, ready to stop me from veering over the road should I fall asleep and lose control. I tried to fight the urge to sleep – I tried to think about as many things as possible, or focus on something up ahead. I even tried working out some distances. Perhaps it was the thought of this maths that sent me to sleep again so quickly, because in no time at all I was asleep again, and I was having dreams about transit horns and Will Collins! My riding became erratic and the team pulled me over and decided it was in fact a good place for a rest. Better to be safe than sorry.

I awoke, again, in quite a panic and was very eager to get back on the bike and keep going. I felt terrible for needing that sleep and again felt like I had been sleeping for days. Often a short sleep of only a few minutes would be enough to fool my brain into thinking it had been rested. I have learned that the most beautiful feeling is battling extreme tiredness and then giving in to it, embracing that wonderful feeling of closed eyes. So peaceful.

I didn't want to arrive at John o'Groats in the dark so I had to press on. I was even more obsessively worried about the schedule and I felt certain that my weakness and unscheduled desperation to stop at Fort William would have caused me to fall behind. I don't enjoy playing catch up; I suffer from the pressure of being behind. I am perhaps my own biggest critic and being behind, to me, meant having to fight even harder. I am not usually driven by a need to avoid failure in fact I usually thrive on a close challenge. But on this ride I was constantly anxious. Being this concerned with failure, I don't think I would have recovered had I have fallen significantly behind. The team tried to reassure me and let me know where I was in relation to the existing record. Although I could hear their answers that I was ten hours ahead, I was unable to accept them; I knew I would only accept an answer when I was back in Land's End. Otherwise there was so much that could happen and jeopardise the outcome.

I was becoming less and less coherent and I was all too aware of it. Occasionally I would correct myself when offering an inappropriate or irrelevant answer to a question, or I would get angry at myself for not being able to verbalise my thoughts. I knew I was breaking down. I was scared that I might break down beyond what my mind could recover. But I hoped that stage was still a long way off and provided the team could put up with my absent mindedness then I would be OK to continue. Alastair was the next person to get frustrated with me. I asked him how far I had to get to John o'Groats. After he gave me his answer, coupled with a reassuring pat on the head, I asked him how far it was to John o'Groats. "Do you think I can get there?" I asked him. "You'd better, because then you've got to get to Land's End again old boy" he replied. I didn't like the sound of that. "So am I close to John o'Groats?! I asked. He looked at me and I knew I had said something wrong. In a slightly exasperated tone he ushered me onwards, telling me I would make it if I just concentrated on moving the pedals.

He still hadn't answered my bloody question!

Loch Ness was my next target. It is such a truly impressive feature of Britain. The Loch itself holds more water than all the other lakes and rivers across Britain put together and is 23 miles in length. I noticed every one of those miles for the road surface is far from ideal, the road is far from flat and the narrow roads meant that huge queues would back log behind me; this was something I had been finding increasingly stressful. I was riding alone past Loch Ness and despite the mounting traffic that I was exposed to, I found the setting peaceful (most likely due to my lack of awareness). It afforded me plenty of time to think.

Inevitably my thoughts turned to the ride and I was now questioning why I was out there on the bike trying to break this record. What was keeping me going? For me, the best explanation for why I was there has been put forward by a man named Andy Kirkpatrick, one of England's greatest (and most entertaining) climbers, who I feel I have a lot in common with when it comes to challenge motivation. The common aspects I see are the addiction to the challenge, and the inability to settle for past experiences. There must always be something more. In his book, 'Psychovertical,' Andy writes: *"It seems that no matter how hard I climbed, the thing that was pushing me on could not be satisfied. On the summit I would feel free of it, but in the days that followed it would creep back. Some people have described it as a rat that gnaws away inside you and must be fed. For me it was something else; it was a rat that denied ever being fed. No matter how hard I climbed, I seemed to have the inability to just be happy with what I'd done. I was always undermining my own achievements"* (Andy Kirkpatrick, 2008). To me this sums up my life, too. I have something inside that keeps yearning for adventure and a challenge and to push myself further and further. When I finished cycling across the USA my first thought was "where next"? I decided that I wanted to go further; to investigate one more road. When I reached the summit of Kilimanjaro I was overjoyed. The scenery and the sense of achievement filled every part of me and I felt as though I'd completed something that might quench my thirst. But then I thought: "which mountain next? How about the seven summits?" The day after completing a marathon I always think "which one next? Can I do it quicker? Can I run further?" I always want to go on to do something better for I also undermine everything I've done. I don't like this about my character for I always remain unsatisfied. Actually I strongly despise it. I wish I could change that about me, but now I think that maybe it is a part of me and who I am. I have yet to work out where it has come from. I wonder whether it is partly dissatisfaction with who I am?

It has only been relatively recently that I have been able to change my attitude regarding how I see myself relative to others. I have come to the realisation that I am exactly what I am, and I am not everyone else; nor will I ever be. I look different, do different things, say different things and think differently because I *am* different. It took a long time for me to realise that, but now I think I have found it. I have found an intrinsic way of dealing with the world – my actions and ideas are thought up by what I am motivated to do intrinsically; not by something that I think other people would value me doing. But that doesn't satisfy my own question about why I seek out these big challenges. As much as I have tried, I have not been able to come up with an answer. It is perhaps something bigger than miles and speeds. Maybe it's about breaking barriers within myself.

Anyway, excuse my short attempt at self-discovery. On with the story.

The small sleep I'd been granted caused me to feel more awake and alive, allowing for a slight improvement in performance and the potential to process the distances and to address the mental preparation for the latter stages of Scotland. Would this enable me to annoy the team less? I had a real focus on John o'Groats and that was my next destination. I longed to see a road sign that said John o'Groats or anything else which might mention the name. I didn't really care for the places in between; I just wanted to be half way. In hindsight, setting John o'Groats was to be a target just too far away.

Sadly for me, it was still a very long way off. I had yet to reach Inverness and although I had moved Inverness in my head to be close to John o'Groats it was still 120 miles away. Those 120 miles were along the coast with an extremely stiff headwind and it was 120 miles with serious, strong, and significant bonks. The bonks were increasing in severity, and more to my concern, they were increasing in frequency. To have this continuing all the way back would be to jeopardise the success. I needed to work out the cause.

Passing through Inverness I was able to navigate myself easily using the road signs, but also the memories that I had from my previous journey. I was on my own and was looking for the large bridge that would take me over the water, off of the A82 and onto the A9. The road became fast and open and the wind speed increased. For once I was grateful for the lorries for momentarily breaking the wind. The road was all ascending too, so although I found this difficult at the time I was looking forward to the return journey. Thankfully the start of that return journey was only 100 miles away, and although that isn't very far in the grand scheme of the ride, I was to learn that it was a long way when embarking on what would be one of the slowest sections of the ride.

It is only right to admit that my body was shutting down and significantly failing on my approach to the half way stage. This was unexpected so early in the ride and was causing much panic for both me and the team. The A9 was unforgiving, the wind adding to my challenge and sapping every piece of energy I could muster into the pedals. I once more had Will join me on the road and his presence caused my emotions to spill over beyond my control. I was aware that Will was immensely strong, and he looked so comfortable on the bike talking me through the route and generally chatting about everything and nothing in particular. I found it absolutely necessary having him or Tony there beside me. I wish their enthusiasm had cycled beside me the whole way. For that time Will and I continued through the gloomy weather of North East Scotland with a stiff headwind and only the small ring on my bike to power me along.

We were descending a long hill just north of Helmsdale when my foot became immensely painful. I could finally feel it again for the first time in several hours. As I was free-wheeling I unclipped my foot to wiggle it around and get some blood back into it. Usually this helps bring back some sense of life, freeing the foot from the confines of the cleat and the pedal. As I removed all the pressure from my foot, it felt as though someone was tearing my foot away from my leg. I felt all the pain concentrated in the ball of my foot. There it seemed to dwell, biding its time until suddenly it would try to escape through the ends of my toes. We were overtaken by a lorry. The noise drowned out my crying and the sudden rush sucked me along the road. I clipped my broken foot back into the pedal and I used the opportunity to get a tow.

I turned to Will only a matter of metres further along and burst into tears. I think he was pretty shocked by my breakdown but, to my surprise, he didn't laugh at me! I felt like this was almost a break through, and he dealt with my emotions very well. I was worried that I'd allowed my pains to surface too significantly for I'd been trying not to acknowledge them, or to at least let 'the other person in my head' deal with them on my behalf. I was petrified I'd lost this control and amid the searing pain I was all too aware of, I doubted whether I'd get that control back again. It was a worrying time, for I knew I wouldn't be able to continue with that level of pain in the forefront of my mind for another 1000 miles.

In a rather subdued manner we continued climbing the next hill and the added pressure to my foot, although painful at first, seemed to numb the intense pain that I was feeling. It became a confusing situation. My foot was causing me agony, but the most comforting way to manage that pain was to push harder on the pedals (not that it had any clear impact on my pace!). I was already fighting a bonk and so I was climbing at a super slow pace. The motor home had driven ahead to Wick and I pictured the town being very close. In fact, I had recurring memories that it would be just around the next corner. I pleaded with Will to let me know *exactly* how far it was to

Wick where I was due to receive my next feed. He didn't answer at first, and left me asking the question with more urgency, then utter desperation. I was frantic to know how far it was; I was really distressed and yet he wouldn't answer.

Finally Will turned to me and said "eight miles, mate...maximum!" That made me really happy; I could last eight miles, although I'd be slow, I could make those eight miles to food. Then we rounded the corner and saw the road sign: 20 miles to Wick! "Shit" I said as it felt like someone was applying my brakes. I couldn't last that long. Not a chance. Feeling let down and helpless I finished that particular climb and rolled off my bike. I had been asking for food for such a long time to try and combat my bonk, but with the motor home so far ahead I wasn't getting anything other than the water on my bike. I was angry, I felt empty and worst of all, I felt useless. Progress was so slow I didn't think I'd ever get there now. I threw the bike onto a patch of grass and then in truly dramatic style I refused to continue riding. I couldn't possibly go on without some food.

My rage lasted only a few seconds before Will, Dan and Alastair distracted me and we started laughing at how terrible the progress was and how desolate the surroundings were. It looked like everyone had packed up and left centuries ago, deserting all the villages. Cold stone walls and drab building work was all that greeted us between the endless foggy fields. It was hardly somewhere I wanted to ride further into. In fact, it was all I could do to continue cycling North – I was desperate to start heading South. Dan started discussing the café that we had stopped opposite. Will described it as "the worst looking café ever" and said "what a stupid place to put a café – somewhere more populated and I am sure it would get a good trade, but round here I bet it gets nothing at all". Dan went to investigate while I sat in the back of the transit and cuddled into the blankets and towels that were available, my body shaking gently as it tried its best to keep me warm. A few moments passed and Dan appeared with two steaming cups of tea that I hoped were stocked with sugars. "That café is well nice on the inside! And he didn't charge me for the tea. Gen up."

I sat for a few more moments, drinking in the warmth of the sweet tea, until I felt a little more human. Following some slapping and anything-but-helpful stretching, my legs felt as though they were going to be capable of more than just a crawling pace, and so I clambered back on the bike. I apologised to it for treating it so badly, but requested that it get me to Wick so I could join the others. Yes I was talking to my bike. The route became much more level in those last few miles before Wick and I was relived to be able to sit down and turn the pedals. Will and I were having more jovial conversations and we were trying to construct a McDonalds in Wick. We passed all manner of big stores and became very excited at the prospect of eating a hot McDonalds. I was still so desperately in need of food, and the thought of a burger and some salty chips really appealed to me. Although all that thinking of food did nothing other than make me even hungrier.

The night was rapidly approaching and I had resigned myself to the fact that I would arrive at John o'Groats in the dark. There truly isn't anything to see up there, so I wasn't too upset by this, but it would have been nice to turn around during the day and without crossing in to the third day. For now, though, I was very much in Wick and I was delighted to have my friend Russ Coles arrive to cycle alongside me. He had flown up and had been staying in a B&B along the route. The team had been in contact with him and he was all set to jump out and join me on the approach to John o'Groats.

I arrived in Wick and saw Pete rushing around in the pouring rain. He greeted with me a careful, supportive hug and told me where I would find the motor home. Whenever I spoke to Pete during the journey, he knew every last detail of what was going on. Everything seemed to work around Pete and he had a calm air about him. His communication was superbly clear and concise and with no more words than were necessary he would give details and advice. At this moment he was trying to get me some hot food and informed me that he and Tom were now charging around all the places that were still open, trying to find something warm. Although I was saddened by the absence of McDonalds (never in my life have I felt this way) I was encouraged by the thoughts of any warm food.

I was taken to Russ' B&B room that was only a few yards away and allowed to sleep for 20 minutes. I was soaked through to the skin resulting from the heavy drizzle, and so changed into some dry, fresh clothes. I slept on the hard floor and woke up to an incredibly calm and relaxed Russ getting dressed into his cycling kit ready for the surge to the half way point. He looked so fresh and strong that I worried I was perhaps wasting his time. I heard him discussing my condition with someone on the phone, and he wasn't holding much back. I heard the words 'wobbly' and 'knackered' and smiled to myself – they were deadly accurate.

I think the next events will remain a joke between me and the support team for years to come, but Alastair appeared with the fruits of the food hunt. I was greeted with a warm, plain jacket potato and a raw carrot. Although not exactly the kind of meal I was hoping for to help me recover from my bonk and prepare me for the second half of the journey it was still food, and that was something I'd not had for what felt like a lifetime. I devoured that potato and the carrot so quickly and with such little thought to chew, that I could feel the burning sensation all the way down to my stomach. Between my teeth was plenty of carrot skin and whilst determined to set off again with clean teeth, I was eager to get back on the bike immediately. Eager that was, until I saw how heavily it was raining.

The rain was lashing down, bouncing off the road and reaching mid way up my wheels yet again. The noise of the rain on my helmet was so loud that Russ had to shout for me to hear him and the constant thumping of the droplets on my neck was instantly irritating. I was wearing dry kit and so I could feel every drop as it made its way down my back; every single cold drop that made its way through the fibres of my multiple layers. I recall that feeling of being tense, trying to stop the cold rain getting through to my skin, and then the sudden relaxation of acceptance. I guess it is most like jumping into the cold sea. The quicker you relax and accept it, the quicker one gets over shock.

I mustn't forget that Russ was also out in this terrible weather so I can't complain too much about suffering, being cold and miserable, and wishing I was tucked up in bed while the bad weather passed. But what the heck, I am going to complain anyway!

I was so wet it was ridiculous. My nether regions

and arse were so soggy that the skin was deteriorating rapidly and the rubbing of my shorts and the saddle meant I was experiencing hellish discomfort. Without any guards on the bike there was nothing I could do to keep my arse dry. I tried to pull the tail of my jacket further down, but as soon as I moved it just jumped up my back and exposed my rear to the rain and the spray off my tyre; that line of spray being directly in line with my arse-crack. My hands were also so soggy that they were badly wrinkled and the continued pressure from leaning on the bars was making them worsen further. I was wearing a pair of winter gloves which Tom had brought along and they were holding my hands together as much as possible, but in no time at all the rain would find its way through every barrier that I could put up.

Russ and I continued on the road, picking up the A99 bound for John o'Groats. I was still extremely tired despite my snooze in Wick and with the added discomfort of the extremely heavy rain I tried to hide in a world away from all the weather. I was relying on Russ to navigate for me, the transit van behind us using its full beams to try and light the road ahead. Again, the road was covered in surface water and the rain seemed like it was never going to relent. Russ was doing his best to sound positive and keep me chatting, but I think we both preferred to just get on with the pedalling without pretending that the job at hand was a pleasant one.

It was refreshing riding with Russ; some new

company while out on the bike was something to keep my mind occupied and ultimately it gave me a chance to reflect on some of the previous events as Russ was asking about the experiences thus far. I was making very little sense and many of my answers were unrelated to the most recent question asked, but I tried to hold a conversation when one had been instigated. I happened to be more concerned about what lay on the road ahead of me.

Filling the carriageway on both sides, and hopping along in their element, hundreds of toads provided a sort of slalom through which I could try and navigate. Unfortunately I didn't avoid them all and I could feel a good number of them splattering up against my leg. Unlike my attempt to avoid them, Russ just continued riding in a straight line, rolling over many of these poor creatures. That was when I first considered the idea that they weren't actually there. Nobody had mentioned them. Perhaps this was the start of my hallucinations? Maybe I was suffering from the lack of sleep more than I thought. I looked across to Russ who appeared wide-awake.

I had been warned several times about the experience of hallucinations and I had experienced several during my training. I hadn't yet superseded my previous experiences of sleep deprivation so I was surprised, but ultimately concerned, that I might be hallucinating already. My usual vision distortions are that road bollards are people and that I can see birds flying around me. Neither of those are frightening or harmful, but I'd never experienced toads filling the road! This was entirely new and that in itself was enough to upset me. There were still several nights of missed sleep to come, so what on earth might I picture later on? For now, my mind, like the road, was full of toads.

The route was still taking in gentle hills and there were several times when Russ and I expressed how nice the turn around would be so we could ride back down these at a more respectable pace with the wind at our backs. Russ is a super strong cyclist. With decades of experience inside his lycra he was trying to drag me through these tough hills, and where possible he would shelter me from the strong cross winds that were battering me along the road. He couldn't do a thing about the rain, however, so we set to moaning about how heavy it actually was.

We discussed this for several moments, and all the while I was thinking about the toads, but there was not a chance that I was going to admit seeing them in case I really was hallucinating. Russ talked about the rain, the wind, the temperature, the hills, the wheels on his bike, his bike lights, his rain jacket, how he was feeling, how I was feeling, but there was no mention of all the toads in the road. That was it – I must have been imagining them. It petrified me. I was yet to reach half way and I had already lost the plot.

We finally turned the last corner and saw John o'Groats ahead of us. I could see the team in the motor home already there and Tom was ready with the camera. It was a great sight again to have the whole team in one place. I remember getting off the bike and falling into the open arms of Ben who gave me the most comforting hug I could have asked for. I felt terrible. I was cognisant that everyone before me had stopped at this point and I didn't want to stay and be added to that list. Ben's hug was perfectly timed. My left knee was in a world of pain, and my foot on the same side was causing me agony. I was once more treated to a talcum powder dusting, but I was eager not to sit around for too long – I would soon get cold which would make the start of the return journey far less pleasant. I also didn't want to spend much time off the bike for my arse to start getting used to the freedom. I needed to keep it firmly in the saddle.

Russ and I were soon back on our less than merry way and heading South. Arriving at John o'Groats unfortunately felt like the finish to me. I had been gearing up for reaching there from the moment I set out from Land's End, perhaps incorrectly. I lost sight of it only being the half way point and since being on the road, and in my desperation to reach there, I imagined (or hoped for) something more like a grand finale. Finally I had made it to John o'Groats. The most desolate and empty part of the British Isles. There were times when I was convinced I would never be able to make it there. The closer I got, the further away it seemed. I was longing to make it to that forgotten patch of land that happened to be as far from the finish as was possible. I call this type of situation a half-way-humdinger.

All that stood in front of me and the record, and the chance to get off that saddle, was doing all of that again. Every single yard of that journey.

Ben Allen and I taking a rest at home in Somerset during one of my final training rides.

After 18 000 miles of preparation.

Ben and I discuss my worries in the lanes near Castle Combe.

Alastair decorating the motor-home.

Will and Tony prepare the van with the spare bikes and equipment before departing my parents' house in Taunton.

That's me stood nervously waiting for 9am to arrive

ost of my support team. From left: Alastair Steel, Tom Emery, Pete ull, Tony Solon, Will Collins, Me, and Dan Tudge. (Not in picture, Ben len and Chloe Felton).

e first few pedal strokes away from the start line (I was searching for e contact with my parents).

Top left; Early, exuberant support along the A30.
Above; The early pace was already starting to hurt me.
Left; The A30 soon ground to a standstill.

Jem Hulse joined the team near Tiverton to keep me company (and make me eat!).

Clive Middleton and Chris Wood join me in the cold, dark and rain through the early hours in the Midlands.

Pete Scull documented every aspect of the ride.

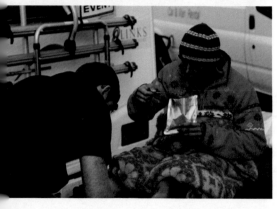

Above left; My first opportunity to have a rest after 24 hours, 100 miles ahead of schedule. Left; After a quick sleep, I was treated to food and massage from Tony. My calf muscles were extremely angry from the cold and wet night ride.

Above; I can still hear the sound of that rickety engine behind me now…

Right; I think this was my attempt at looking happy after 700 miles.

Above; I rolled to a stop at John o'Groats and could no longer control my emotions. My head was full of toads…

Left; The swelling in my legs made walking extremely painful.

Above; The team gathered at the half-way point (Note how sleepy we all look).

Below; At the top of Shap my body was starting to shut down. Will had some very stern words to keep me pedalling.

Above; Alongside Loch Ness. Tom said, "Smile and look like you're enjoying this". This was the best I could manage.

I actually have no recollection of this. It is during one of my 'absent minded' episodes where I made predictions and recounted childhood memories.

Tony feeding me a mixture of fruits, oat bars and chicken pieces.

Dan and I salute the team as we approach the climb to Rannoch Moor.

If you look very closely at the road you'll see Dan and I dwarfed by the mountains around us.

After the hell of bonking through the Great Glen, the team bury me in blankets to give me a sleep and a massage (Bon Jovi was blasting out the stereo and locals looked on in horror at what was happening).

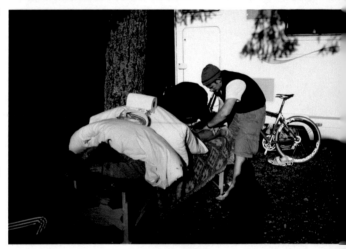

Russ Coles kept me company through some of the worst rain

Above; Nobody besides the team and I on the road in Southern Scotland. My Exposure MAXX-D Light shining brightly.

Left; Will and I riding through a long period of silence.

Tom Emery with an ever-cheery smile stuck on his face.

Chloe managed to join us in Monmouth. I can't remember a time I've been that happy to see some-one.

Right; Richard Bates (far left) with the members of The Bicycle Chain who weren't out on the road with me.

Below; Roadside support from friends near Taunton.

Right; The number of people joining my ride grew and grew as we passed through the South West of England.

After a final 10-mile time-trial effort, the team engulfed me for an emotional embrace.

The whole team enjoyed the closing moments – the goal was achieved.

Less fresh-faced than six days ago.

taying awake for breakfast with the team and my family in Penzance
as not possible. I spent several days like this.

ly wonderful parents, Paul and Trudi.
hank you for your perfect support."

5.

"With ordinary talent and extraordinary perseverance, all things are attainable"
(T.F. Buxton)

Ever since I started training for the ride I had not wanted to stop at John o'Groats. I wanted to arrive there, cycle past the sign with a well timed photograph to prove that I was there, and then continue on my way immediately. I feared John o'Groats. It seemed the cemetery of LEJOGLE attempts and by stopping there I felt I was searching for my grave. So with the excitement from the team, Pete's gentle words, Ben's regional abuse and Tony's shrill and piercing cheers, I was soon on my way back, relieved that I would at least escape the vice-like grip that the car park had on my mind.

It was 23:00 and I was leaving John o'Groats, not a moment too early, heading south for the first time on this journey. Before rolling away from that desolate place I received a final comforting hug from Ben and further supportive words from Pete who never lost his faith (or so it appeared) in my ability to make it back on time. Neither did his enthusiasm or energy wane at all in almost 2000 miles – quite a remarkable man. The rain was still extremely heavy, but in my favour was the same wind that I had battled on the way north.

It meant I now had a healthy assistance from

behind, pushing me home, and coupled with the large number of descents, I picked up a very good pace. I no longer had a computer on my bike, so I was left guessing my speed, or more accurately, nagging Russ to give me a figure. Often I longed for it to be breaking 20mph, for then I would really feel like I was making some decent progress. Yet there were many times when I was unable to maintain that pace and had I had confirmation of my slow speed, I would have been harsher on myself for slacking. I was hungry to get as far away from John o'Groats as I could, but more so, I was desperate to get back to Land's End.

My physical ailments were almost becoming too much for me to cope with. I was in a great deal of physical and emotional pain, and my mind continually revisited the memory of the other riders that had attempted this record and stopped at John o'Groats.

My body was very much depleted and mentally I was doubtful whether I would be able to survive the return journey. The northbound journey was one of the longest, sustained competitive rides I had ever done, and I had been forced to ride that in truly terrible weather conditions. I so desperately wanted to see Chloe and have some treatment; I imagined her healing hands getting to work on my legs and my back and fixing whatever problems were there. I sought reassurance from the waking members of the team, trying to figure out if I had enough left in my reserves, or if they had enough faith left that I might be able to borrow some. Approaching the very real concern of my failure made me cry. I just wanted something to take the pain away. I asked if the swelling in my hands would hinder the progress, or whether my knees looked like they were jumping or stabbing at the pedals. I was concerned with my form. It actually felt as though pieces of my body were breaking away from me, and I was being left with only the useless parts that didn't propel the bike. Pete really had a great eye for delivering motivating comments, passing them over at just the right times. He saw every perfect opportunity to read me some of the many, many messages that were still continually flooding in. This alone lifted my spirits and amidst the tears brought a tremendous smile to my face; a smile far more powerful than any of the painkillers, for it seemed to fill my legs with a sense of happiness. I listened to an answer phone message from my dear friends Maurice and Maureen and their excitement over the team reaching the half way point so far ahead of schedule made me grin from ear to ear. I used their enthusiasm to get me back on track and bound for the Westcountry.

After a sombre start, Russ and I eventually settled into a comfortable pace and we were eating away at the miles. He very slowly turned to me and uttered perhaps the most encouraging thought through the entire ride: "Every town you pass through now is crossed off the list. You don't have to go through them again, they're done. Its all on the way home now". I kept this thought in my mind and it spurred me on to 'check off' each of the towns. That was to become my method for working through the country, and I praised myself when I managed to check off some of the more major ones that I considered big milestones. Inevitably, the more tired I became the greater the number of 'significant' milestones I created! I needed something to make me feel like I was progressing. I would pester the team in order to find out the name of the upcoming towns and work towards crossing them off my list. Each time I managed it, I would be closer to the end. I also wanted a countdown on the miles.

One thing still troubled me though, as I rolled away from the Northern most point of the British Isles. There were still hundreds and hundreds of toads in the road. I asked Russ how he was getting along, hoping he would make some reference to them. Again we discussed the weather, what lay ahead and all manner of things as we had encountered on the way up. Finally, and almost as though he knew I was waiting on it, he said: "and there are a load of toads aren't there". I felt such a surge of relief. I actually wanted to laugh with relief, but I decided that that too would make me seem a little unsteady. I was tired and didn't know how I could react! At least my mind hadn't constructed the whole thing.

With that relief I almost felt relaxed. Russ was just a cruel bastard for riding over them! The pace increased as I relaxed and I was able to cycle without that major concern looming over me. I remembered each of the long climbs that I had fought with Will's and Tony's company on the way up and longed for the ease of riding down them now. Russ was engaging me in as much conversation as possible; discussing our plans to cycle to Portugal the following summer. I dreamed of the warmer weather and used it as a mask for the heavy rain that was still thundering down on our backs. I was unable to wear my glasses any more – the weather conditions overwhelming their ability to dissipate the water on the lenses. We discussed the physical problems that I was having and whether I thought they might get any better between there and the finish. I thought it was perhaps a ridiculous topic because there was of course, no chance of these problems getting any better. They were with me until the bitter end, wherever that was.

Russ and I were riding deeper into the night so there was the added battle of my extreme tiredness. Having fallen asleep in the saddle next to Will, the team was conscious of taking extra care to keep me awake. I am a regular bed timer at 22:30, and although I'd seriously altered my sleeping patterns in training, something still made my brain crave a pillow at this time every night. For several hours I struggled with the desire to sleep, reducing my pace and stopping all verbal communication, or at least reducing it to one-word responses – my best effort at being talkative! Looking back at the experience now, I am extremely grateful to Will, Dan, Tony and Russ for their remarkable efforts at keeping me talking at these times of minimal response. I know I was more communicative inside my head, but they continued to talk to me (at me) about all manner of topics and with faultless enthusiasm about their subjects. Some of them ought to consider talking for a living. Will, perhaps, should not. These four managed to extend my riding time quite considerably and although there are many sections of the ride that I now fail to remember, it is through the events and interactions with these four people that I often link things together. But that didn't always work. Sometimes I was too confused for anything to make sense.

My brain was performing quite a dance between reality and fantasy in response to the tiredness and the physical fatigue I was going through. It appeared to give me pleasant, comforting, almost relaxing thoughts and visions before snatching them from me and leaving me to fester with panic in the grim reality of what I was doing. Grasping the truth of the experience was becoming intensely problematic.

We were descending towards Helmsdale on a very long and gradual descent, the road flanked with utter darkness, when my thoughts turned away from the wind that was caressing my face and I became aware that Russ was no longer beside me. Instead, there was a white van driving very slowly behind me, despite having ample room to over take. I became aware of the noise from the engine as though it had just been turned on, like the sudden starting of an old diesel generator. It broke what I

thought had been a complete silence. There was also very little traffic on the road, so there seemed no obvious reason why the van didn't overtake. I beckoned the van to pass me, which it duly started to do and I looked forward to having the quiet world return once more.

It pulled alongside, and then to my surprise it was filled with people I recognised! (In hindsight, this was clearly a moment of mental instability. My brain was working without conscious understanding of what I was doing.) I thought my friends in the van would perhaps know where Russ had gone, but before I could say anything, they informed me that he had cycled back to the motor home to exchange his lights. They then said he would be with me shortly. While I was delighted that Russ would return, I was still uncertain why they were there, and why were they helping Russ? Why were all these people I knew in a van following me during the middle of the night while I was on my bike? What was really going on, and what had they done with Russ?

Frightened by my lack of understanding and what they'd done with my friend, I climbed out the saddle and increased my pace. I felt bad for cycling so slowly if Russ was in need of help. I thought that he must be ahead of me, so I attempted to find him before the van did. In my mind the faces of those people inside were friendly, but I couldn't work out why they were there? Nothing was making sense. I was pedalling hard, working my legs very aggressively. I powered over a slight undulation and felt thrilled with the sudden speed that I was carrying; but I still hadn't found Russ. I thought I had to save him from these people, but I was failing to reach him. I didn't think I would ever catch up. In my worry, I then considered the idea that Russ had perhaps disappeared completely, but then swung to the thought that I'd only imagined him ever being there.

Then, very casually, he just re-appeared alongside me, continuing a conversation, presumably from where he'd left it. To be honest, I wasn't aware he'd been talking about anything in particular, so I tried to be polite and offer my single word replies at breaks in the talking where it seemed appropriate. I don't remember being outwardly excited, but I was so relieved to have found him again. Only now, he seemed very concerned about me and how I was feeling.

Russ's riding increasingly started to reflect his anxiety of me falling asleep and disappearing over the edge of the road. He positioned himself very close beside me, easily within touching distance, and he continually checked to see how I was feeling. It was becoming apparent that I took my micro sleeps on any descent unless I was actively engaged in something – eating, drinking, chatting or trying to work something out. If there was a break in conversation, or if I took too long to verbalise my responses, Russ would say "ok Ben?" or "still awake Ben?" He would actually ask this at very regular intervals: a maximum of 20 seconds apart. At first it made me smile, the regularity of these checks, but then as I started to fall asleep between them, I realised it was actually serving a pretty important function. I laughed when I was mid sentence and Russ interrupted with "still awake Ben?" Perhaps I should have started returning the questions!

The tiredness finally took over and on one descent I completely fell asleep. My legs were still going round but I was firmly in the land of nod. I woke up many moments later to the sound of excessive beeps on the horn and a very concerned Russ looking at me, after he'd been desperately trying to wake me up. Sensing the danger it was decided that I had to be pulled off the bike. I was granted a 20-minute sleep at the side of the road. I felt extremely cold, and although I was happy to be on the return journey, I couldn't help but feel like there was a serious mountain ahead of me still. I started to doubt myself.

By the time I awoke, I was facing the last few

hours until dawn. Russ was already set and raring to keep me company again, safe in the knowledge that after my sleep I would be more awake and would continue to increase my pace and interaction in conjunction with the rising of the sun. Russ was still wearing the same cold and wet kit that he'd started riding with, so I can't begin to imagine how cold and worn out he must have been feeling. For now the weather had eased off and the rain had taken a rest. The best feeling for me was getting myself into something dry. Frustratingly, every time I changed my shorts though, I changed the outermost layer of skin on my arse. Changing the shorts meant peeling the current shorts away from the broken and bleeding skin of my backside and then carefully placing the new pad for maximum comfort. I hated doing this.

Fortunately the sky was reasonably clear after that short sleep and Russ and I were able to watch the colours in the sky grow lighter and the day's light appeared over the distant horizon. Seeing the sun come up each morning was such a relief. It signalled to me a complete day of riding in the light, but more so, it signalled the end of one more night. I longed for the day's light to make everything operate more smoothly. I enjoyed being able to pick visual targets and check them off more regularly.

Russ jumped into the motor home just before Ardullie where the A9 crosses the water. I remember this event with utmost clarity for it was where I had my first 'accident'. I had been cycling alone for a few miles since

Russ had departed when I felt an overwhelming need to use the toilet! I am still unsure why, given my extreme meal of a jacket potato and a carrot that I had such a strong and sudden urge, but it was causing my stomach to cramp and I needed to solve the issue as soon as possible. Unfortunately my hands were now completely numb and I lacked control over each of the digits. This made tasks such as gripping zips, or pulling at shoulder straps impossible. I was stuck in my clothes. My neck muscles were also starting to fail (Shermer's Neck) so I was unable to retrieve items from my jersey pockets. I was ultimately stuck on the handlebars. I radioed the motor home and said I needed to stop and use the toilet. "I've got five minutes at best before I need you to be here". They were further back the road sorting Russ, feeding him and getting him dried after his long stint in the saddle. Their reply: "You're gonna have to wait at least twenty minutes before we can catch you." I calmly replied: "you'll need to get a clean pair of shorts ready then please". Cycling with an unhappy tummy is far more difficult that one might imagine. Leaning forwards whilst having the pressure from the saddle at the same time makes the whole experience far worse. There is only one option when that happens; only one option if you wish to continue cycling anyway. Nature called.

The motor home appeared just the other side of the water so I wasn't left with my accident about my person for too long. We pulled into the first layby and I was given a few moments to clean myself up. Although another hindrance to progress, this was an essential stop as continuing to ride in that state could have caused some serious troubles further down the line. The degrading skin quality and the sores that were already in that region would have become far worse if I'd left it much longer before getting cleaned up. This stop came half way through the final climb before Inverness. I knew from the top of that climb I would have a gradual descent and fast roads all the way to Inverness. I relished the thought of faster riding, and that carried me to the crest of the hill and powered me along, searching for urban images of Inverness. The feeling of being able to 'power along' when on the bike is something only really noticeable when you're unable to do it. I can only describe it as being able to choose when and for how long you wish to ride faster. Sometimes it is more a state of mind and simply involves applying more force, perhaps through a bigger gear. At other times it might be getting out the saddle and feeling each of the muscle groups doing their job in pulling you to the crest of the climb. That's what it is like for me, anyway. I can only describe that off the back of not having that ability for many miles at a time.

The long open road of the A9 gave me a fast re-approach to Inverness. The traffic was pretty heavy as we were navigating the city and I quickly lost the support vans who were trying their best to shout directions to me. I had Dan out on the bike trying to navigate for me, but I was able to do the job myself. The sunlight made a world of difference. While Dan was tracking back to check directions with the support vehicles I nipped off through the traffic jam and made my way through the city and back onto the A82, heading back to the banks of Loch Ness. Russ was asleep in the motor home, catching up on some shut eye having spent the night out in the cold with me. His total effort from Wick was an extremely helpful 140 miles ridden in some of the worst conditions I have cycled through. Without his company I am sure I would have fallen asleep, veered off the side of the road, resigned myself to utter despair at the conditions or become so insular in my approach that I wouldn't have said a word to anyone.

I cycled the length of Loch Ness without any communications, but with the motor home close by so I could have regular chats and updates about my progress if desired. These updates were becoming increasingly routine and the same details would be spouted by whoever happened to be in the nearest window. Tony would always give me details, which were 'on the nose'. He appeared, in my presence at least, to have a crazily strong certainty that I would make it to Land's End. How could he be so sure? Had he not been listening to me when I told him what was falling off and out of my body? Whatever was going on, these updates made me feel much more capable and in control, but I knew I was progressively getting slower. I could no longer feel the constant pain in my foot. It appeared as occasional pain, injecting the ball of my foot with excruciating precision, culminating in a shout of discomfort before it all disappeared again, and instead I could ride and think about another part of my body that was slowly breaking down. Tom went past hanging out the window with the camera poised and the instructions "smile and look like you're enjoying this". The result was something of a horrified, half-tortured expression; I could think of many more enjoyable things to be doing!

I started to complain in the last few miles of Loch Ness about a growing sense of hunger. I couldn't really remember anything other than the carrot that I had been given in Wick on the northbound journey and I was eager for something that I kept calling 'proper food'. I longed for a hot meal, or something that would take me away from the monotony of energy food and chicken wraps that I had been eating on the way up.

Tortelloni was something I craved, but Lasagne and Cottage pie also featured very highly on my wish list. I cycled into Fort Augustus, a place of many memories from my previous journey from end to end and I wished now for the relaxed pace and laughter that I shared on that journey. I wasn't enjoying this ride anymore and all sensible decisions would have been to quit and get home in the van.

I am so glad not a single person in the team was feeling sensible. This time as I entered Fort Augustus there was an abundance of coaches with tourists. Dan squeezed the motor home between several of these coaches and inside I was treated to lasagne, chips, cauliflower, broccoli and countless salted crisps by way of fuelling me for my challenging section ahead. It was almost perfect. I ate myself to a completely full state and could barely fit anything more in. The team found this meal as a psychological boost rather than a nutritionally crafted meal. It did offer me all that I needed, but by stopping and being given some 'proper' food I felt for a second that I had left the ride and was somewhere different. It was the first time I felt like I could get away from it all and I was upset that my portion of lasagne was getting smaller. I wanted to eat as much as I could to prevent another bonk, but also to fuel me for the long climb up to Rannoch Moor which I was constructing in my mind as some sort of vertical wall that I was expected to leap over. It stood before me in my mind, posing a serious threat to the future of this attempt and Dan was all too aware of it.

I jumped back on the bike feeling utterly stuffed. I had actually turned away food before I left the motor home, certain that I couldn't eat anything else. I rode along the road for only a couple of miles before, very frustratingly, extreme hunger suddenly struck me again. It now seemed like I was fighting a battle with my metabolism to absorb the calories that I was putting into it. I had suffered significantly more bonks than I had been expecting or hoping and myself, like the team, were anxious of the damage these bonks were making to the clock. Each time a bonk appeared it would run through the same patterns. I would start to slow, complain about hunger, feel extremely weak throughout my body, and then get what I have always called the 'sugar shakes' in my thighs. When this happens it feels as though nothing connects my feet to my thighs and each remaining drop of energy gets lost to the surroundings before it can be directed through the cranks. At their worst, bonks lead me to a total feeling of vulnerability that just screams for sleep.

Fortunately, if that's the right way to look at it, I couldn't feel my feet by that time, so that feeling of disconnectedness between my feet and thighs didn't impact upon me, but over and over I would battle with my body wanting to give in. I was now in new territory, physically. I had never cycled this far without a 'real' break, so the events that now lay before me I had not encountered before. How was my body going to react to more riding, but no more sleep? How would my mind deal with the task that lay before me? I was keen to discover the answers, but I was keen to do so with the reassurance that things could be mended. I longed for a physio session and a massage. Everything was hurting and I frequently experienced spasms in my thighs. I wondered if this was from nervous system conditions or just nutrient deficiency.

I sat in the saddle, evaluating myself and my performance and my very reasons for being in the saddle. I struggled to rationalise the reasons why I was still there, for I hadn't been enjoying it for quite some time and I was suffering some really terrible injuries. As a totally honest answer, and one which we're perhaps not meant to admit, part of the reason I kept going was the worry of quitting and letting people down; I didn't want to be perceived as a quitter. Another detail that passed through my mind was the regret that I would undoubtedly feel if I had chosen to get off the saddle. I was into the second half and the 'miles for' were growing way faster than the 'miles still to go' increasing their difference all the while. I had passed my halfway humdinger so giving up seemed rather silly. I drifted along, often freewheeling while I thought about this. I ran some of the messages I'd received over in my mind and tried to imagine other people sitting at home and tracking the ride from their computers, clicking refresh to move the red dot further along their map. I was smiling at the thought of that, but longed to be there instead.

Then I received another message from my motivational guru, David Badger. I had cycled with Badge for the first time in the Crudwell 24 hour race back in the June of 2010 and ever since I had been motivated by his crazy enthusiasm and positivity. He had been sending countless messages at all hours around the clock, sometimes with stories, sometimes with jokes, sometimes with wise words of inspiration. He sent a very personal message about the impact that the ride was having on those people around him - it actually started me crying. I was blubbing at the image that that particular personal message had created in my mind. But it was perfect and perfectly timed and I was delighted he'd shared it with me. It changed my focus to a more proactive and believing viewpoint where I could see myself riding and wanted to ride more. I was on an adventure and the best part - it was motivating other people to undertake their own adventures too.

Entering this new territory immediately altered my outlook. It took my anxiety and disposed of it and gave me the lift in my spirit that we'd all been searching for. Sensing a new adventure and the opportunity to take my mind and body to a new level of functioning (I'll leave you to decide whether that is a higher or lower level of functioning) motivated me to learn from the experience. I combined my inexperience of something on this scale with the 'checking off' of the towns as Russ had said. I had a target and a neatly constructed ladder from which I could reach my destination. Sure, some of the rungs were far apart while others were only a small shuffle, but each one was a step closer to the end; a step closer to breaking six days and twenty hours.

I pressed on from Fort Augustus with Rannoch Moor at the forefront of my aspirations. I made a terrible estimation error, thinking that it was pretty close; instead I had an imposing series of hills ahead of me before such time as I'd reach Rannoch Moor. Sensing hills, Will jumped out beside me and we were busy chatting away, and for once, able to enjoy a turn of good weather. I can only assume that Will had had some good sleep because he was on top form and was chatting more rubbish than a dustbin man – exactly what I wanted him there to do. I didn't even resent him for talking about how comfortable the bed was, or how warm he felt when he woke from a long sleep. I didn't even mind when he talked about the food and the drink that he'd had just before getting out. I was just happy that he was spinning beside me with hours worth of talking stored up inside him. We laughed at my broken body and at the task I was putting it through. I found that laughing helped belittle the challenge.

I recall somewhere on the route near Fort William, the exact position I can neither confirm nor deny, but it was somewhere in that region when Will decided that I wasn't cycling fast enough! He based that decision on the fact that I was overtaken by a man on a tourer with a pannier attached to the back of his bike. I was quite happy to let the man go – he clearly had more energy than me. However, Will Collins knows only one way to ride, and that is 'putting the hammer down' particularly when someone else is looking. So as Will cycled right up to the touring cyclist, sitting on his wheel, he turned around and demanded that I kept up. The words he uttered are perhaps best left to guess work, but they left me in no doubt that I was not to be passed and dropped by a man on a touring bike, especially seeing as he was loaded with panniers. But they were 50 meters ahead of me; I could never catch up!

We were on a marginal incline and I recall pumping at the cranks with complete determination to pass this other rider. My legs were aching, my muscles filling with contempt for what I was suddenly asking of them. My lungs were burning and my mouth resembled a drought. I could see Will riding with a huge grin on his face, looking over his shoulder to make sure I was putting in enough effort. My effort was increasing with every turn of the pedals, but my pace wasn't changing in the slightest! The intense race-like chase continued for several hundred meters before the touring man pulled off the road into a layby on the left. His decision to stop meant I was finally moving faster than him. In fact I was gaining on him rapidly. I pulled level with him. A small expression of delight spread over my face as we made eye contact. I passed him. I was winning.

Big endurance rides require these small victories.

The sun was still shining as the day matured. Ok, so I'm being slightly dishonest. The true weather report was that it stopped raining, but I like to see the potential in these events. Identifying his opportunity to get in some miles on the bike alongside me, Dan decided to jump out, fully armed with food. Lemon slices, banana, cereal bars, High5 energy drink, and the secret weapon (unbeknown to me at that point), the trusty mars bar, all filled his pockets as more dry miles were added to Dan's support tally.

We passed through several small settlements nestled into available land space alongside Loch Linnhe. Dan was doing a great job as domestique, feeding me with a good amount of food and encouraging me to get fluids into my system ahead of the big climb that we knew was approaching. I was busy taking small nibbles from my lemon slice, not eating too much in one go owing to the poor condition of my tongue and my mouth. Large quantities of food aggravated the splits in my tongue and the rest of my mouth was so dry, that chewing food became extremely challenging.

As a child I would often dangle my tongue outside my mouth, give it a quick rub with my sleeve and then leave it outside my mouth for a few minutes until such time as it had dried out. I would then pop it back in my mouth and find the texture really intriguing. Slightly odd, hey? But this is what had happened to the entire of my mouth as a result of riding for so long with my mouth open. The lining of my cheeks and palate were raw and my tongue itself was covered in splits that would swell and bleed. The food I was consuming was so painful that I started to miss food intakes, or 'drop' most of it on the floor (a totally stupid thing to do). I couldn't lubricate any of the food, so I was suffering from the friction as it dragged its way down into my stomach. At times I resorted to filling my mouth with strepsils, sucking on them for a minute to numb my mouth, then filling it with food and washing it down as quickly as possible.

I was just finishing up my second lemon slice when I looked up to see a large red bus attempting to turn left at the roundabout. The only problem being that he was in the right hand lane. Dan had already arrived at the roundabout in the correct lane, ahead of the bus, hoping to give me a clear run through without yielding for traffic. This procedure had worked on every roundabout so far – the support rider or vehicle advancing to the roundabout, entering the roundabout system and then arriving in time for me to just jump out ahead of them. It also enabled me to see where I was going. Only this time, the large red bus decided that it wanted to drive over the path that Dan was taking. An entertaining, but very heated exchange, consisting of heavy taps to the side of the bus in between blasts on the horn, was shared between Dan and the driver. It is the first time I have ever seen a bus change its course following a shove from a cyclist.

In a split second, Dan turned to me, checking I made it through the route detail successfully, but with utmost calm. He was very cool and collected and began briefing me on the major climb that I was about to face. He completely kept that outburst away from me and we didn't discuss it. We flanked Loch Leven together, still deep in the process of getting food into my system. My little burst with Will had placed too many demands on my system (I prefer to blame him than my ability) and I was fearful of the onset of another bonk. The last place I needed to fall prey to yet another bonk was at the bottom of the climb, or indeed anytime before the summit of Rannoch Moor. I passed through the small Glencoe village and there before me stood what I considered to be a behemoth mountain climb.

The ascent is really only a gentle grade. Looking back at it, the climb isn't that significant – merely long. Ordinarily this would be my perfect kind of hill climb, something I could attack, but on this day it turned out to be my downfall. The sun was warm and heated me through the black leg and arm warmers that covered my limbs. I was also wearing a thick winter jersey that acted as an incubator to keep my body heat inside. I'd lost all control over my fingers by now so I was hopeless at undressing so I resigned myself to an uncomfortably warm climb. I managed to roll one leg warmer down to my ankle, offering me just the suggestion of ventilation.

Hindsight truly is a wonderful tool. Not only does it allow us to relive the experiences that we have had, but it also allows us to learn from them, gaining better understanding of our actual experiences or the real situation that may have existed unbeknown to us at the time. As I sit and recount the events that were involved in that section of the ride I see a multitude of mental strategies and emotional failings to blame for the severe drop in performance. I had been so worried about the recurring bonk and how devastating it would be at this particular time. Coupled with that, I was significantly over-estimating the challenge of this climb. Those two factors caused me to 'talk myself out of the climb'. I bottled it. I ambled up the climb, reluctantly putting effort through the pedals. The hill had beaten me without me even putting up a fight.

I believe Dan was aware of this. Dan was actually aware of a great deal more than I was. He and I had no contact with either support van, and as a result, we had no food supplies near to us, and certainly no insurance for a mechanical failure – bike or body. Dan acted supremely over the course of the next 35 miles. In that time I was completely without the support vehicles. Dan suggested I needed to pedal a lot harder as I could have been dropping time against the standing record. It was the first time he'd said anything seriously about me falling behind. Panic and confusion surged through my head – had I really dropped all the time I had made on the way North?

How could I ever get back to that pace now? I was horrified and wanted to put this right. I worked *for* Dan up that hill.

His motivation and words of encouragement were perfectly suited to how I was feeling at that precise time. There was no messing around and no friendly words. He made me ride faster because that is what I had to do. I became angry and frustrated at the lack of food. I wanted to know where they were and how long it would be until our paths crossed. I was angry because the support vehicles had abandoned me, and I didn't know if I could ever make it to where they were. Dan let me see him share that anger, acknowledging my frustrations, but then talked me into the strategy of how *we* were going to get through it. He allowed me to feel as though we were both going through that particular strife and I was appreciative of that. He didn't deny me the right to feel that way and to that end, he helped me accept and deal with the problem.

As Dan and I approached the top of the ascent we then faced the long and exposed sections of the A82. Dan still harassed me to ride at a much higher tempo. I knew I had been comparatively coasting up the hill from Glencoe, but Dan was keen for me to capitalise on the post-climb miles. I needed to increase my pace and make up for the previous fifteen miles at such slow speeds. I battled so hard with the task and I expressed to Dan continually that I thought I was going to have to give up. He replied with "you're definitely going to do this, mate. Not doing it is not an option". We continued riding, spending much of our time searching for a glimpse of one of the support vehicles. They'd driven on ahead. Too far ahead.

It was more a mental breakdown, but this feeling of abandonment and the inability to make contact with them left me feeling helpless and in danger. I rapidly deteriorated and was depending on Dan for even the most basic of needs. I kept letting out little whimpers as my knees buckled under my body weight, and every time my back would spasm my hips locked in place, preventing me from turning the pedals. My body was truly failing me – I'd lost feeling in my feet (one of them broken), my hands were completely numb and useless, my neck had stopped working as it should leaving my arms only able to function in front of my body. Everything between my belly and thighs had become numb during the climb, which obviously helped with the pains in my arse. I'd become urinary-incontinent and had lost all feeling in my genitals, my perineum (the gooch), and thankfully the sores on my arse. My mouth was so dry that my tongue had split, the lining of my mouth progressively more stripped away by the rough food stuffs that I was piling in. My left eye wasn't focusing and both my knees were so swollen that I could feel the pressure of the fluid building up with every push of the pedals. The last thing I needed was to be hungry and abandoned by the support vehicles.

Regrettably, I became angry towards Dan. He was my only outlet for why I found myself in this situation, and I blamed him (who else could I blame) for getting me so isolated. I finally managed to push him for a detail, but I think he offered it as a gesture to pull me through. I so desperately needed some information regarding the distances before me to help form a plan in my mind. This section had been too long without a known target and I was suffering severely because of it. I needed a rung on my South-bound ladder and Dan told me the rest of the team were in the next town. Too tired to realise that he was purely hoping, rather than conveying fact, I latched onto that information and immediately started assessing my condition, urging myself to continue to Tyndrum – the next village on the route. I was so in need of a rest, and my body was in desperate need of some more food. Throughout this account of the ride I keep describing each subsequent bonk as the worst I'd experienced, but at that point I really was in the middle of one of the worst bonks I'd had all ride. It was physical and mental.

Therefore the last thing I needed was to roll through Tyndrum to find no sign of the team at all. They weren't there. I'd given everything I thought I had left in me just to get there. They had to be there. I couldn't go any further. Why weren't they there? Dan told me they would be and I could have some food and some treatment on my legs, but they weren't. I had no option but to keep pedalling. My brain had already stopped. It stopped as soon as I entered Tyndrum and my emotions started to get the better of me. I was so hungry, yet everything seemed irrelevant now. My mind stopped supporting me and I was down to my last energy reserves. They had to be in Crianlarich.

Dan remembers: "I recall chatting to Ben and trying to encourage him to go a little faster. Why I was telling him to go quicker I will never know. I found it pretty hard to gauge what was encouraging and what was annoying. I explained to Ben that he needed to concentrate on turning the pedals. He must have hated it! But I really didn't know what to say.

Things went from bad to worse, to awful. We had ridden a fair old distance uphill and Ben was tiring. I did my best to encourage him but he was ruined. Again, it is difficult trying to spur on someone in such a terrible state. Unfortunately the van and the motor home had gone ahead. Ben required feeding but they had decided to push on and find somewhere suitable to stop. Also, I had no radio at this point, perhaps the only place along the ride that I hadn't had one on me. It was a bad move. Ben hit the wall big time and was in a seriously bad way. I kept telling him just a little further, just the next village...and every time we got to a village, there was no sign of the crew. I was thinking it was stupid. No radio, no support and Ben was probably at the lowest point of the ride in terms of energy. I felt terrible for him. All I wanted to do was push him! But, of course, I couldn't. I tried to feed Ben half a mars bar at one point. He refused. I thought about it for a second: here is a man that is out of energy but he doesn't want to eat! I gave it about 10 seconds before saying to Ben: "here you go, eat this". He seemed to get it - there was no protest whatsoever.

We passed through another village where there was still no sign of them. I considered leaving Ben at the side of the road and going to find the support crew. I decided against it, though. I knew they had to be really close; it was just a shame that for Ben it was about 10 miles too far. The only saving grace is that it was now relatively flat. When we arrived with the support crew, Ben was broken - physically and mentally in ruins. He broke down."

Without Dan being there, I would most likely still be on the side of the road at the bottom of the climb from Glencoe. Dan kept me going through each of those miles. He spurred me on and offered the most perfect words to keep the pedals turning around. I felt in a juxtaposition needing emotional support on one hand and a kick up the arse on the other; Dan seemed to deliver both at the same time. He is a man of many wise words. The disappointment at not finding the team in Tyndrum was all too evident on his face, too. He was equally angry with the distance which opened between us and was determined to make damn sure that it wouldn't happen again.

The miles from Tyndrum to Crianlarich were filled with absolute minimal conversation. I needed to be off the bike and I desperately required something to eat. I rolled into Crianlarich, thankful of the minor descent, to see the motor home parked in a gravel lot at the side of the road. Dan guided me in. I came to an eventual stop, my fingers battling to pull the brake levers, before slowly rolling my hips over the saddle. I tossed the bike away in an outburst of helpless emotion and waddled off to find a private space behind a tree. I didn't feel I could face anyone without bursting into tears. I was emotionally rock-bottom, which just added pressure to the simultaneous physical collapse I was experiencing.

Ben and Pete ambled over to chat to me, and being the very first face I saw, I opened my anger on Ben. Although with hindsight we look back and laugh at my misplaced outburst, I feel terrible for unleashing my anger on Ben. He was not responsible for the situation. In fact I blamed him for feeding me only a baked potato and a carrot at Wick! Something he had had nothing to do with. Other than hunger, I don't quite understand the relevance to that particular outburst, but this is where it surfaced and Ben just happened to be the target nearest to me. As I sat at the base of the tree, my head hanging between my knees, I allowed the tears to come pouring out. A lump that size in my throat would ordinarily affect my voice, but right then such a quivering effect would have gone unnoticed. The lump consumed my throat, and with the release of the tears came a release in the tension that had been contorting my insides for so long.

I was finally admitting to myself that perhaps my body had suffered too much. Resulting from my extensive training, I had become extremely effective at over-riding my physical pains during performance, but this was an entirely new level. I was unable to convince my brain that my body *had* to keep working. Ben and Pete crouched beside me. I felt beyond help; totally dependent on them to get me out of this situation. But I couldn't see how. Their comforting hands on my back said more than any words, and I felt secure in the knowledge that they were now back with me. It wasn't just Dan and I out on that relentless climb any more.

That comforting moment ended when a firm hand appeared on my shoulder. "Ben. You've got two minutes to get yourself together. Then I want you over on the massage table for some food, treatment and a sleep. Quick as you can." The firm hand was unmistakable. Dan wanted to make sure he sorted me out from this situation. He handled my emotional wreck flawlessly and in just a couple of minutes the team were gathered around the massage table, sharing messages, food, stories, jokes and toilet humour while Bon Jovi played in the background as motivation for the next recovery and continuation. Bon Jovi wasn't just a random choice of music; it was one of the groups to which I often listen when training indoors or during spin classes. I associated the songs with physical power – something I frantically needed to find!

I lay on that massage table talking to the team about how malicious that climb had been. Will laughed and called me all sorts of names, but still offered me plenty of food. There was some sort of team competition taking place, trying to work out which bit of food, and from whom, I might take handfuls next. Will admitted defeat with Bourneville chocolate – that was never going to win. I did, however, get the chance to express my disappointment with the last section and berated Dan for his commanding assertiveness at pushing me up the hill.

It was a similar rallying situation to the one back in Cumnock on the northbound journey – the whole team were gathered around and we were able to recharge our energies and ideas about how to progress from that point. The first thing I needed to do was get to sleep and shake off the effects of that bonk, so amid the hullabaloo of food and Tony's massaging hands, I was buried under a mountain of cushions, blankets and jackets and left out under the open sky for my longest period of shut eye.

It still wasn't enough.

By the time I surfaced from that one hour sleep,

the darkness had signalled its approach and I was ready to embark on the next night ride – my last period of night on the northern side of the border. I set out with the intention of not stopping until past Glasgow where Russ Coles was due to catch a plane home to the Westcountry. Unfortunately I stopped a matter of minutes later and tore off lots of my clothing. I woke up feeling very chilly and was concerned for how I would manage the cold for the rest of the night. I overdressed considerably so almost right away I had to hop off, strip off, then hop back on, leaving Tom with the lovely, fragrant kit that I'd removed. Someone has since told me to always 'be bold and start cold'. I felt completely different to how I had before my rest and meal. My mind felt more agile and positive, my body felt a little more relaxed, and the chance to laugh with the team made me feel more at ease with the cycling. I now felt human again and as though my body was there to work. I gained strong control over my emotions once more and felt more positive about the forthcoming miles. By all accounts there wasn't much climbing between Crianlarich and the Erskine Bridge so I felt immediately better knowing that my knees might get a little rest from the mounting pressure developing inside them.

It probably goes without saying, but when I say I felt 'better' again or I felt 'refuelled', the standard I'm referring to was getting progressively lower. What I considered strong or alert was getting worse and worse.

The fifty miles that followed were rapidly counted

off, resulting from a much-increased average speed and a better road surface to see me along. Although I had multiple lights on the front of the bike, I still needed the help from the vehicles behind.

Russ decided he'd had enough just short of the Erskine Bridge, so he hopped back into the van and was whisked off to the airport for his return journey. I was battling with tiredness, but with enough food I was able to maintain reasonable conversation. I was, however, increasingly concerned about my knees. I had developed an irritating 'clicking' action and a sensation of grinding from deep within my knee, and the fluid which was once in my knee was spreading down my leg and into my ankle. During my growing years I had had numerous issues with my knees and frequent dislocations, so I was used to unpleasant events happening to my knees, but this was something different – this didn't feel good at all.

Dan joined me where Russ left and together we rode for an hour, discussing what would happen if we were stopped by the police; about the visibility of his helmet lights and about a million hypothetical situations all before heading over the Erskine Bridge. I remember riding beside Dan at this moment with great clarity, for I associate those miles with extreme pain throughout my entire body. My limbs were experiencing a continual burning, throbbing pain much as though a hot pokers had replaced my bones. My throat and my mouth were preventing me from swallowing comfortably, and to that end, I was repeatedly trying to clear my throat of the viscous, pungent goo that I was producing in place of saliva. The bags under my eyes and the weight in my eyelids stood testament to the fatigue that had now commandeered my mind. Despite the jovial nature with which Dan and I tried to converse, my body was slowly ceasing to function. What scared me the most was that I had lost control of my thoughts, too.

Crossing the Erskine Bridge is where my memory of the ride vanishes. In fact, over the course of the next 100 miles, the challenge of the ride proved to be too much for my mental composure. I 'lost the plot' as I crossed the Erskine, behaving in very concerning and unusual ways. I have extremely sparse and vague memories of reaching Gretna, the English border, but the period between is a total blank. I feel robbed of the experience and saddened at missing such a significant event in my mind's experience. I wish I could have experienced the turmoil that my brain and body were going through. I will tell the stories of Glasgow to Gretna with the help of the memories from the support crew:

Dan and I had opted to take the cycle path rather than the main road across the bridge. While I'd made this decision and thought it a good idea at the time, Dan was unsure why we'd left the quiet, empty road to ride on this poor and puncture-likely rough path away from the headlamps of the van. He was right to be unsure of the decision. We battled a strong cross wind that was blowing through the bridge; the pair of us out the saddle trying to maintain some sort of pace against this barrage of strong gusts. Using some unorthodox and unstable riding we re-routed back onto the main road and for the major roundabout that would send us back towards Glasgow. I turned to Dan and enquired if he remembered ever being there with me before. With a slight element of concern in his voice he answered: "yes, I remember. We passed through here on the way up". I corrected his reply and pushed him to recall the time that we'd cycled through there when we were much younger; when we were small children. Dan was unsure what to say, but rather than dispute my certainty, Dan simply said, "oh right, yeah, maybe". Be aware that I have only known Dan for a couple of years, so there was no chance that what I said held any amount of truth.

I then embarked on a lengthy demonstration of how well I knew the area. I seemed convinced that I had been there before, and that I had already lived through the events that were unfolding before us. I claimed to have known every pothole in the road and every sign that indicated my directions. I even went as far as professing to know which cars would overtake me! It had all happened before, but when probed I couldn't quite remember what the result of it had been. I became anxious, desperately trying to work out what was happening and why I was reliving this part of my life.

Amid this battle inside my head, trying to figure

reality from memory, I was very much aware of the racing speed of my heart. I kept telling Dan that it was beating like a dormouse. It was beating so fast, but it felt exceptionally weak. I lacked any ability to ride fast; the slightest exertion making me feel so weak. I was moving so slowly and staring at the world around me with wide open, fearful, confused eyes. Dan allowed me to express my thoughts without challenging them. Instead he tried to help me understand what was going on, and took his time to explain details about the ride that I was actually in the middle of completing. Of course, I already knew everything that he was telling me. I'd done it before, hadn't I?! Ahead of me, the motor home had pulled off the road, parked neatly beside the transit where the entire team was prepared and ready to greet me. Dan had radioed ahead to warn them of my current state, and the team was on standby to receive this confused and broken individual.

Dan recounts: "It was particularly concerning when Ben went mad. I had been cycling with him and chatting about all sorts on the way down through Glasgow. He seemed to be in great spirits, but it soon became clear that, although he had energy and was pedalling, he was mentally unstable."

According to Alastair, I readily pulled up alongside the vans, jumped off my bike, leaning it against the side of the motor home, saying hello to each of the team as I saw them. I was cold so I announced that I would sit in the motor home to try and keep warm. Unlike all the previous stops since my body had been failing me, I walked without so much as a limp; I climbed the steps into the motor home without any trouble and I tore off my cold and wet clothing all by myself. I sat down at the table and expressed my concern about this recurring deja vous that I was experiencing. I tried to stress that I knew what was going on owing to the fact that it had all happened before. Alastair and Tony were stood beside me while Tom used the opportunity to squeeze in some 'interesting' filming: Dan had wanted to capture the cuckoo on camera! Tony reports that I was very matter of fact and stated the issues that were concerning me, but making very little sense at the same time. I had a cup of tea made for me by travelling chef, Pete, and some cookies to try and give me some energy. At this stage Alastair was trying to work out what was going on with me, and Tony phoned his brother for some psychiatric advice. Of all the places to crack and fail, why had I chosen Glasgow?

The story of events then grew even more unusual. I borrowed a pen from the record keeping sheets, and started writing on my palms. I was very secretive about what I was writing, refusing to let anybody in the team see what I was predicting. I leaned tightly into the corner of the van, taking care to conceal my hands from all angles; I needed to show them I'd been there before. I wanted to prove to the team that I had actually experienced this exact situation and the best way to do that was to predict what was about to happen. The detail I wrote on my hand was that one of us would be stopped by the police. There appeared an obsession with the police. It later unfolded that none of us were stopped by the police. But I remained adamant that somebody would be.

I then grew very concerned about my bike being left outside. I didn't trust the area that we were in and was convinced that someone was going to steal the bike. How then, would I make it to Land's End? Ben reports that I was very anxious and demanded that he kept an eye on the bikes. Even when Ben was stood out there with the bikes, I turned to Pete and requested that he also keep watch over them. I was paranoid.

My thoughts started to jump through all manner of random events. A man cycled past on the street just outside the door of the van and I grew angry that I had been overtaken by someone else on a bike. What if he made it back quicker than I could? I didn't want that; I suddenly wanted to be back on the bike and making some more progress. It was so important to me that I prove to the team how I'd been through all this before. I was still really cold, and so I asked Pete to grab my infamous yellow rain jacket from the transit in an attempt to keep a little warmer. Pete disappeared and hadn't come back before Ben was holding my coat, offering to help me put it on. According to Ben, I looked at him intensely, saying with a confused look and slightly angry tone in my voice: "I asked Pete to get me that". What was I becoming?! At first I was reluctant to accept the coat, given that Pete hadn't handed it to me. Eventually I gave in to Ben's offering and I popped it on before getting back outside, again with an apparent absence of physical ailments. It was time for Dan to get some sleep, so Tony decided to hop on the bike beside me and try to make some sense of what was going on in my mind.

However, he didn't manage this without just a little confusion on my behalf. Tony was busy getting himself dressed and ready to assume riding watch-duty beside me when I turned to Pete and asked in a most confused tone, why he was getting dressed into cycling kit. Pete reports that I was really troubled and struggled to understand why he'd be getting ready to ride his bike. I said: "why is he [Tony] getting changed? Is he going to be cheering or something?" Pete was unsure what to say or think and was, himself, utterly bemused by the situation. It was a relief for the rest of the team when I was back out the van.

Tony's report said: "Ben was now at a completely different level of exhaustion – something I had never witnessed before. I immediately realised it was going to be a major struggle to keep him awake. I tried all of the tricks I had up my sleeve to keep him alert. We cycled along singing Bon Jovi tunes and trying to remember the lyrics to others for a couple of hours. We had a few enjoyable conversations about star constellations and the Universe. However he started to verbally ramble quite a bit suggesting that we were cycling in circles and that we had already cycled down the roads we were on.

I thought he was astutely realising that we were cycling South on the same road on which we cycled North, but in fact he continuously believed that we were cycling repetitively on the same sections of road again and again. I wasn't sure how to deal with this and started to criticise myself for not studying how to negotiate someone's sleep deprivation whilst preparing for the challenge. Amongst the apparent utter exhaustion, Ben displayed brief moments of amazing lucidness, given the circumstances. As we were cycling through one town he amazed, and kind of scared, me when he stopped and got off his bike very randomly. I was wondering what the hell was going on – I had no idea what he was up to. He had seen a traffic cone on the road which had fallen over – Ben decided that this needed to be rectified and walked back to it, stood it up and moved it in off the road – hilarious given that moments before he was wobbling on his bike struggling to stay awake! On another occasion we had a conversation that went along the lines of:

Ben: *"have you any money?"*

Tony: *"Yeah Ben, I always carry a few quid on rides as you know...why?!"*

Ben: *"Hmmmm I'm quite hungry, I want real food, I think I'll go to that shop over there and buy a tuna sandwich"* {gesturing to the hedge on the right hand side of the road}

Tony: {looking around and seeing nothing but dark

countryside, hedges and the night sky – realising that this is a complete hallucination I decided it best to play along}

"OK Ben, no problem… but you know those shops usually have pretty crap sandwiches – why don't we get some food from the camper van instead?"

Ben: *"OK, that sounds fine, when will that be?"*

Tony: *"We can get them to stop in the next town when I'll get some food for you"*

{situation resolved!}

{about 5 minutes pass}

Ben: *"I'm very tired"*

Tony: *"OK, how tired? On a scale of 1 to 10?"*

Ben: {completely ignoring my question} *"I think I'll just lie down here for a while and have a rest"* {gesturing at the ditch on the left hand side of the road}

Tony: *"Ahhh… I don't think that's a good idea Ben, we can get the camper to stop in the next town if you think you need to sleep for a while?"*

Ben: *"Sure, you cycle on ahead and I'll catch you up in the morning"*

Tony: *"We can get the camper to stop in the next town so you can sleep in it."*

Ben: *"No you go ahead with the vans, I'll rest here and I'll catch you up tomorrow"*

At this point I realised the true extent of his exhaustion."

Tony was understandably becoming more and more concerned. I showed little, if any, comprehension of the task at hand, and I failed to place the names of people who were submitting messages to the team – even family. I wasn't responding appropriately, and I failed to understand his simple instructions.

A police car pulled alongside us (not an hallucination – an actual police car!), and looked through the window at what was going on. Ah ha! I knew it, I had predicted this. This is where one of us would be stopped. I was certain. I had just started blurting out my prediction to Tony when the police car drove off and we didn't see it again. Ok, so it wasn't at this point – but further along the route it would happen. We just had to wait for it.

What I wasn't prepared to wait for, however, was a sleep and some food. I needed both of them right then. I didn't want to wait a moment longer. So why couldn't I have them? I have a lot of respect for Tony for how he kept me on the bike at this time, and kept me pedalling on the right route to make it South. Without his thought to try and understand me and my experiences at that moment, I wonder whether we'd have continued. It sounds like I was putting forward every reason why I should be off the bike, construing all manner of creative and innovative reasons, yet he kept riding beside me, guiding me along the road that would get me home. He tried to understand what was going on in my mind and why I had suddenly changed from tired, but making sense, to completely illogical, incomprehensible, and certain that I was reliving my own past. This cannot have been an easy task at all.

We were descending a relatively quick slope into the outskirts of Kilmarnock where there had been some minor road works. Although we were travelling at over 20 mph, I started cycling directly at another road bollard that was across my side of the lane. Tony shouted at me, thinking I had failed to see the bollard, and worried that I might crash into it and fall off my bike. At that speed I am sure I would have sustained at least some level of injury, whether I would have been aware of it or not. Instead, I got very close to the bollard before anchoring on the brakes, bringing my bike to a sharp and sudden stop and giving quite a shock to the van travelling behind me. I leaned off my bike, picked up the bollard and then tossed it off the side of the road! Tony just laughed, perhaps with significant relief, and said "well done, mate; very good of you. Let's keep cycling now, shall we?"

I battled with the condition I refer to as 'cuckoo' for just over another hour before I finally rolled up to a patch of road where I was overjoyed to see the motor home parked up. I raced inside, keen to get warm, have some food and some sleep. Owing to their concerns about the state of my mental condition and a result of the advice they'd sought, the team allowed me to have a decent sleep, tucked up in warm blankets. It was a delight, and I was full of warm food and hot drink. I was out like a light with minimal time for chatting. I simply wanted to get some more sleep and finally my head made the perfect marriage with the vast quantity of pillows that filled the bottom bunk of the motor home.

The 'cuckoo' episode has been explained as my brain going into a protective state where it was stopping me from experiencing the nasty reality that I was putting it through. My body was experiencing so much pain that my brain could no longer deal with the dissonance between recognising the pain on one hand and then making my body continue cycling against its strong pain detection. To appease the situation, my brain entered a state of exhausted shut down where it was making my reality my memory. That way it could bypass the reality and not have to deal with the pain that was overwhelming my senses. This is why everything I was doing felt as though it was happening for the second time in my life. As soon as something happened it was interpreted as memory! I desperately needed to sleep and let my senses rest.

I woke half an hour later in fabulous pain. My body was smarting all over, nowhere more so than my knees and thighs. They burned with the angry acidic feel of anaerobic exercise, and were tender in much the same way as suffering severe DOMS. Just to the touch, they caused me anguish, and Dan's vigorous massage style made me think that getting back on the bike might have been a more relaxing idea! The team seemed happy that I was in pain once more. They welcomed me back from my venture into the other world inside my mind, for all of a sudden the broken ruin that they had been guiding south had returned, albeit in a far more grumpy and tired condition than before.

Tony was charged with the responsibility of riding beside me once more and we cycled through the last few hours of darkness before the team welcomed the arrival of the day's light. The sun brought a new dose of joy with it that morning for it decorated the scenery with a frosty, misty, bright but impending sense of hope for the day ahead. Tony and I discussed the cattle that were in the roadside fields and how much I was looking forward to getting back and visiting Maurice and Maureen on the farm. I longed for a relaxing day where I could be in the fields working at various tasks and spending the entire time looking at nature. That feeling seemed so far away. The mist lingered in the valley off to our left and for several hours, Tony and I shared a peaceful, relaxed spin along a very quiet section of the A76. The road surface was decent, the traffic situation quiet, the views absolutely wonderful, and the atmosphere among the team was relaxed.

Many of the team-members have expressed how the mist clouding the valley matched their worry clouding my mental state. Although I appeared to be back on the progressive path of deterioration, many felt the end of me would arrive before the end of the ride. I was unaware of this at the time, but having heard their accounts of the ride, there was a serious question surrounding whether they would let me continue. I like to think I would refute their decision to admit defeat, but caught up in the pain and the distress of the situation I am concerned how I would actually have responded.

Silence was very much the order of the day along the A76 as I progressed much slower than hoped towards the English border. I was still alongside Tony who was performing miracles to keep me pedalling, to keep me eating, and to keep me drinking. I'd stopped doing all three, and together they are rather essential to the maintenance of progression on a bike. Despite my reluctance to eat or drink anything, Tony persisted and kept me fed and watered as much as he could around my outbursts and refusals. He was forced to take on a very different role alongside me; not an easy role at all, for I was rude, uncommunicative and when I did respond, I was argumentative at best.

The greatest challenge came when we picked up the A75 from Dumfries to Gretna. By this time of the morning, traffic consisted of commuters and lorry drivers – people who wanted to get places quickly. The road was filled with lorries and the noise was too much for me to take. Their engines filled my ears and their shuffling of the gears filled me with a growing sense of anxiety – I was riding so slowly. The team and I were causing some serious traffic delays and many of the drivers unleashed their frustrations when they finally found an opportunity to overtake. I can't say I blamed them, but I had also grown desensitised to their abuse. I was too tired to care. They could say what they wanted. I had neither the energy nor the impulse to retaliate. I just wanted to get off this torturous section of road. There were sharp climbs, strong winds, huge lorries passing close by, no food other than oat bars available, and I was still in Scotland. I complained of another approaching bonk and I could sense it would be a mighty big one; the shakes had come on straight away. In my mind I was watching myself from outside my body, I had insufficient strength to move my gear shifters and jumping out the saddle made me slower. It was going to be a serious bonk.

I sulked beside Tony who fed me every last ounce of food he could. I was tired of the mundane taste of the oat bars so Tony was feeding me bits of chicken. Anything would be better than nothing. I fought harder than ever before to make it to Gretna – back to England. This was a colossal milestone in the whole event, and the more that bonk approached, the more significant the English border became. I'd been in Scotland for such a long period of time and I needed to escape. Mentally, I would be much stronger if I could be back in England and start to geographically locate the places at which I was arriving.

I was now riding in the gutter of the road, which is yet another testament to the Bontrager race-lite tyres I was using, for they still had not picked up a single puncture in the entire ride. Tony was riding tight to the white line so that we were minimising our interference with the traffic, which ultimately meant we were pretty close together. It was evident that the stress from the traffic accumulation was bothering me and so the support vehicles drove in a manner we called leapfrogging, pulling over to allow traffic to progress as much as possible, but also to offer me a sense of distance. This leapfrogging also reduced my feelings of isolation – it reminded me I wasn't on the road alone. I continually checked distances with Tony, adjusting my target every time. Gretna was now the only place I needed to get to; the rest of the route I would think about afterwards, but nothing more for now. Ten miles was all I could handle. Fortunately we were only that far from Gretna, so from somewhere Tony mustered the strength to jockey me into Gretna where sunshine, bacon and egg rolls, and a comfortable pavement were awaiting my arrival.

6.

"Success seems to be largely a matter of hanging on when others would let go."
(W. Feather)

I enjoy reading the team's accounts of the events that occurred during my period of absent-mindedness and the way the support crew continued with their roles of making me ride the bike. Their actions speak volumes in the way they were able to remain focused on their given task and to somehow draw the necessary from me while being in such a broken mental and physical state.

Crossing back into England felt like a gigantic step toward the completion of the ride. I felt as though I was away from the painful, never ending roads of Scotland, and I was able to start counting down the remaining miles. Having cycled 1200 miles thus far, the thought of another 500 didn't sound too difficult. Not as a number, anyway. I knew that 500 miles was still a significant distance, but it sounded much less in my head than what I had done. I compared it, foolishly, to the 420 miles I'd cycled in my first 24 hours. These final 500 would take considerably longer.

With my second egg and bacon roll already repeating on me, Will and I set off from the side of the street at Gretna and headed for the North of England. Spirits were high amongst the team and the warm sunshine (yes, we finally got some more!) brought a strengthened sense of anticipation. With the excitement and enthusiasm that was oozing from Will after his being cooped in the van for so long, we turned the pedals with energy. We turned them so vigorously that we went the wrong way. Only a small error though for I was quickly turned around and left chasing after Will who was shooting off on the correct road.

I learned, just as we were setting off on the right route, that the motor home had suffered a puncture further up the road. Lost in a world of despair and pity I had been oblivious. The team's mechanic, Ben, had had to fix it and the team had to try and keep this news away from me. I admired how they managed to keep such troubles away from my attention until they had been resolved. Their decision to operate in this fashion stopped any unnecessary worry being passed on to me, leaving me simply to worry about cycling. However, with the knowledge of my poor state of mind and my continual confusion throughout the course of events that happened between Glasgow and Gretna, I don't think they had too much difficulty keeping anything from me!

Will and I set out and maintained a sprightly 17mph from Gretna, once again picking up the route change as suggested to us by Geoff Davis on the northbound journey. This new road flanked the M6 and was relatively flat. It meant I was able to make it to Carlisle easily and this, without doubt, saved time and miles from the final count. Although my failing body was still very apparent, I felt I was getting stronger as the day was moving by. It helped having the jovial character of Will beside me, for his turn of conversation and his knowledge of how I respond to discomfort helped me deal with my troubles and motivations. I took the opportunity to offload all my latest concerns about how my body was holding up, and he rode with me very sympathetically, reminding me that I was actually cycling slower than the really old people he used to guide through the Alps. Right then he described me as the slowest yet. It sure does sound like Will was always giving me a hard time or throwing out insulting comments or making me feel really useless. Well in all honesty, he was. And that is Will. But it is the way that Will dishes this out that makes it very reassuring to hear, and in fact, very motivational and relaxing at the same time. In being like this he was once again doing his job.

I recall chatting to Dan about how Will, Dan and I came to know each other and be such close friends. He summed it up very neatly, but very accurately. He said something like "we outdo each other in a supportive way, and we put each other down in an encouraging way. We enjoy hurting and pushing ourselves and each other beyond what we're capable of, while never acknowledging how impressed we are with another's performance; even though we can easily tell. We support each other completely, and although we will never admit it, we each want to see the other two achieve. I think this is why we are so close."

I am sitting here trying to recall the feelings that were passing through my mind and body during that part of the ride, and while I describe myself as feeling 'stronger', I look back now and realise how relative that feeling of strength must have been. I was utterly exhausted and my performance was rolling further and further downhill. I remember my inability to remember; being unable to recall lists or directions myself. I needed short and simple details without any ambiguity, and I required the repetition of these numerous times. I failed to work out the most simple of maths sums, or answer the most basic questions, including personal information. I was totally focused on chipping away at the towns left on the list, and I craved knowledge of the approaching place names on the route. But how could I remember them?

Tony thought of ways to help my memory. While I know it was angering me to be so forgetful, it was clearly driving the team to insanity having to answer my same questions over and over. Often I would ask one, wait a moment, then ask the person beside them for confirmation! Tony came up with an idea to help me memorise details. He started to tell me little patterns of towns that were approaching. At this stage I settled for 'People Kan Like People'. Penrith, Kendal, Lancaster, Preston. Simple – People Kan Like People. Had I been more awake, I think I would have asked for a better construction given the error of Kan. But at the time I liked it, and so now I shall stick by it.

Will was busy unwrapping some food for me just past Carlisle when I told him that my body was about to bonk. Yes, again! I was getting less and less warning of these episodes and this particular one crept up like a prowling tiger. Although he was helpful and compassionate Will found them funny. He found it amusing on the one hand to see me hit rock bottom in a matter of minutes, moaning and struggling, but frustrating on the other hand to have to cycle so slowly beside me. He started ferrying food from the van, dropping back to load his pockets before catching me up and handing out the spoils of food and drink. I had sailed past the stage where food was too painful to eat so I just had to ignore my mouth and throat, instead focusing on the food being in my belly. I struggled with this. I attempted to forget the food being in my mouth, but regardless of how much I focused on my belly, it was still so painful chewing and swallowing. I started to drink strong bottles of fruit smoothie in an attempt to fuel me before hitting the edge of the Lakes. Dan and Tom were in the transit van behind us. Their navigation was impeccable and they were keeping me on the right track and headed towards Penrith, occasionally thumping the horn, pulling alongside and greeting me with huge smiles.

I wanted to express to them that I was struggling. I am sure they were fully aware, but I wanted to tell them myself. I tried to shout at them, but my throat was so sore and my mouth was so dry and cracked, that my voice had different ideas. It was nothing more than a quiet whisper. I failed to form words; I failed to produce saliva! Will joked about the state of my voice, but even my laugh was inaudible. I think he thought I was ignoring him. Who could blame me if I was?! I started trying to point at things that I required, but often this proved ineffective. I was now unable to express my thoughts and needs, so I was fully at the mercy of the team who were left to work out what bargaining tools and what food stuffs would keep me on track. Regretfully, they opted for too many oat bars. It was a real pleasure to experience the mutual understanding that exists in the friendship between Tom and I. Despite my absent voice, I could convey pretty much everything I wanted to with a quick glance; almost as though he could read my expressions. Seeing Tom's face in the window provided that instant relief, like finding your keys already in your pocket at that same moment you fear you've locked yourself out. It was one of those safety feelings that make you smile.

The rollercoaster ride into Penrith forced me to climb out the saddle. I would try and make the occasional break on Will and drop him, but as soon as he started pedalling again he would be flying past me, the offensive comments being the only thing I could keep up with! I dreamed of hot food and begged for the team to have a proper meal ready for when we arrived at Penrith. Rightly so, they told me I had to keep going, and that I couldn't have another break just yet. Reluctantly, I continued pedalling – returning some of the abuse. Not that anyone could make any sense of it of course! I do now, however, realise just how frustrating it is when the person you are insulting or trying to argue with simply smiles and laughs. It is infuriating but at the same times removes all ability to think nasty thoughts. So thank you for that learning experience, team.

I was making slow, sobbing progress toward the Lakes. I was aware that I had Shap ahead of me to climb and I figured I would be stood up, out the saddle for the most of it. Indeed, I'd been out the saddle for so long, throwing my bike around and gritting my teeth so hard to try and ignore the blistering pain in my knees and my neck and there was so much left to climb. My knees felt as though they were breaking, being chipped away, piece by piece and replaced with fire. My thighs were doing the damage and they continued their tearing, electrifying pains each time I asked them to contract. My neck was offering nothing more than the discomfort one might feel having been in the same position for almost five days. It was allowing me an uninterrupted view of the road under my bike, but remained disgruntled whenever I wanted to look up or to the side. I was all too aware of developing full blown Shermer's neck. Little I did was helping, and I lacked all capacity of thought to reduce the climb to smaller, more manageable targets. I stuck with the summit as my ultimate goal, with the hope of catching the van that remained only just in my sights.

I attempted to release some pain by trying to shout at the top of my voice. My outburst didn't help. To be honest, it wouldn't have disturbed anyone in the University Library. Not a sound left my mouth. A quick release of air escaped but not the slightest decipherable word. My voice had truly disappeared. I slumped into the saddle, straightening my back as much I could and dropped the chain into my smallest gear. I started spinning the pedals, making super slow progress – the very same hill as before had beaten me again.

I reached the top looking forlorn and sorry for myself. Some strangers on the opposite side of the road shouted words of encouragement, but I was too tired to say anything back. I recall hearing them, but even failed to offer a smile of gratitude. Instead I mustered a half hearted clenching of my face and judging by their expressions I am sure they doubted what we were actually undertaking. Owing to the difficulty of the climb I had been hoping to have a stop and some time to recover, but I decided with the team's unwelcoming stance that I needed to keep going. I didn't actually want to get off the bike; I just wanted the pain to stop and be taken away. I started the most disappointing descent of the ride. Having fought for so long to reach the summit, I pictured in my mind's eye, a long, continuous and fast descent, where I would barely need to pedal. This didn't happen, and I spent much of my time climbing little humps in the road that were just too big to be carried over by the previous descending momentum. I was perhaps more exhausted on this descent of Shap, but the 'unfair' bumps brought back memories of the Ozark mountains in the Midwest of America – the enjoyable down hill being too little to coast over the following climb. What a lazy mindset.

I continued down the 'descent' and headed along the A6, continuing toward the next town in my little acronym. Kan – Kendal. Seeing the signs for Kendal made navigation very easy. I also had plenty of broken opportunity during the descent to give my legs some massage and a good stretch. I thumped my painful areas with my numb and clumsy hands. It wasn't much of a massage, but at least I was getting something. The stretching was perhaps the most enjoyable. I pushed my heels toward the road, stretching my calf muscles within an inch of their life. I then leaned over the bars and tended to my hamstrings. They felt better for the simple acknowledgement that they were there; I hadn't forgotten them and all their hard work. I encouraged myself to drink in the spectacular views and smiled at the abundance of greenery that was before my eyes. I enjoyed the scenery and took the opportunity to embrace where I was.

I used the occasional increase in speed during the descent to forget about the team and talk to myself. I reassessed my situation with some updated details and worked out that if I picked up my performance I might still be ok for the record. I was all too aware that my position ahead of the record was coming into question and along the current rate of performance decrease I would soon be fighting a huge battle against the clock. I was desperate to get to the end of my acronym. People – Preston. I rolled along the A6 putting a little more pace into the ride, forgoing the pain in my knees. They would eventually heal. Discussions with Pete and Tom helped me so much and I was relieved when they'd appear and start talking – I was happy to just pedal and listen to the highly random thoughts which popped out. I cycled through Kendal, a town in which, during my 2005 ride, I was unable to find any Kendal mint cake at all, and then continued on to Lancaster. My increasingly undulating blood sugar levels hit a huge trough. I didn't recognise the area that we were passing through. Will even told me that he had no idea either! I was expecting him to know exactly where we were, which now, I see is totally unreasonable, but at the time I was angry that he didn't have a GPS knowledge of this town. How could he have directed me to this place without any confirmation from the support team? The answer – we'd lost all communications so Will was doing the best job he could.

Feelings of rock bottom were encroaching again, and as I cycled more miles, the bottom seemed to extend so there were new depths at which I could hit this sorry place. I was suffering from mental bottoms as well as physical bottoms. Fortunately my actual bottom was feeling nothing. But I once again hit desperation on the approach to Lancaster. We stopped in the small town of Slyne – the same place we'd stopped after 24 hours on the way up. On the approach to the village I asked Will how far it was, and more specifically, where in the country this damned place was. I got the usual response: "further along here. Cycle quicker and you'll get there sooner." I rolled along the road at such a slow pace, perhaps 12 mph. I even knew it was slow, but my legs felt as empty as a drum. There was barely any force to help my legs around. I was angry at myself for being so useless. I was angry at yet another bonk.

I pulled off the road to where the team was positioned and I decided I needed space away from my bike. I wandered around the team expressing my concerns and trying to gather information from them. Had they given up and lost faith in the ride? Had I taken on too much, and here in this car park was where I would realise it? I was only 420 miles from the end. So close! I took myself away from the bike and sought some answers. I needed to convince myself that I would recover and be ok.

I managed to get hold of my mobile phone. It was the first time I'd had private access to it since starting the ride so there were hundreds and hundreds of messages available for me to read. Instead I resorted to calling the one person who I thought would be able to sort me out and reassure me that I was making progress. Oh yes, I'd stopped believing my team – I was cycling so super slowly that there was no way I could still be on target, despite them telling me that I was. I couldn't accept their unwavering belief.

So I phoned my very straight talking mother. I took the phone and hobbled away from the others. I wanted a real kick up the arse to stop me from feeling so sorry for myself. I fumbled with the phone, my hands not really working as they should. I managed to press the green 'call' button and held the phone against my head. When Mum answered I was unable to talk. For the first time in what felt like a lifetime, I could feel some fluid in my face and slowly the tears tumbled down my cheeks. I tried to tell her that I didn't think I could make it. I listed the problems with my body:

My feet were numb, although at times extremely painful.

My knees were so swollen I'd never seen them so big – the joints were grinding and constantly clicking and sending such sharp pains through my thighs.

My upper thighs were numb.

My testicles had disappeared inside me, the rest of that area now thankfully void of all feeling.

My neck was so painful that I couldn't lift my head without severe discomfort.

My shoulders had stopped working, preventing me from properly using my arms.

My tongue was split, my mouth stripped and my

voice non-existent (yes I still continued with the whispering call!!!).

My left eye was unable to focus properly.

Apart from that I was in pretty good shape, and perhaps the fittest I have ever been. My Mum did a wonderful job of reassuring me. So good, that I sadly can't remember it. I seemed to drown out the rest of the call with my sobbing and frustration at being so useless, but I left the call with a desire to be back on the bike. So I guess Mum had done just the right job. Since the completion of the ride, I have learned that as a result of that phone call, mum didn't sleep until I crossed the finish line. I worried her sufficiently that all she wanted was to see me off the bike.

I also learned that soon after I was back on the bike and making (still slow) progress, my mother phoned the support crew to establish what was really going on. She admitted that she could barely hear a word I was saying during my desperate plea for help. Depicting enough to give me an appropriate response must have been quite a challenge, but perhaps it is best if she didn't hear all the details at that time – I can't imagine it is what a mother wants to hear. Pete informed her that I was at the lowest I had been all ride, and that everything was starting to take its toll. The team became more and more concerned and without ever showing it to me, they started questioning whether I would make it back. Despite them always hiding this doubt, and never letting me see anything other than positive faces and attitudes, they did decide that I'd gone far enough, and through enough strife without a physio that they needed to locate someone who might be able to patch up some of the injuries.

I kept making progress. I cycled through Lancaster and I was greeted with some lifesaving news: The team had managed to locate a physio who would be able to offer me some treatment in Preston. Although I was suffering a great deal, my mind took this lifeline and made a real effort to get to Preston. Will took me on quite a tour of the city. We zig-zagged through lots of the residential areas and repeated several of the roads. Will was riding with the radio in his ear and was receiving instructions for where we might find this physio centre. The riding became more like an urban time trial as we jumped up and down kerbs, nipped through little back streets and behind blocks of garages. I don't know why I didn't get frustrated with the faffing; I think I was just delighted at everyone's efforts to get me to the right place. We met a man at one set of traffic lights who asked where we were headed. I was unable to offer anything coherent, so Will explained we were destined for Land's End. The exchange went something like this:

Man: What you doing then lads?

Will: End to end if he keeps on pedalling.

Man: Oh right, me too. When did you start? Can I ride with you?

Will: We started at 9am on Saturday… Yeah, if

you like.

Man: Saturday? Oh, right? I didn't see you up there.

Will: Oh no, we started at Land's End.

Man: And you're going back to Land's End?

Will: Yeah, we've been up there already; it's a horrible place.

Man: Oh.

We clocked a McDonalds in the corner of a car park and joked about how wonderful some food from the golden arches would be. Over the radio came the instruction that we were somehow in the right place, and so we raced through the car park to the opposite corner where the team were already tucking into some food and hot drinks. I was so grateful when a box of hot food appeared before me and I was able to wolf down the tasty burger, interspersed with the satisfying salty taste of the chips.

I was taken into the sports centre by Dan who had already been in to discuss with the physio how we were getting on and to explain some of the troubles we were having. I looked like someone who had been cooped up in lycra for five days, cycling non-stop in some of the worst weather without washing, or attending to personal hygiene. To add to that, I had terrible sores inside that lycra, my ability to talk and make sense about my issues was non-existent and when asked questions about my body I answered between snoozes and dribbling. I think it is safe to say that most people who Nicky Argles had treated had been more presentable than I was, but she set to work without any hesitation, despite the fact that we were well outside the normal working hours. I will always be grateful for her extreme efforts and would like to make it clear to her, just how important her intervention was for me completing that ride.

My most fond memory from during that session, besides having my muscles stretched for the first time during the ride and also having my legs 'sorted' whilst being asleep, was waking to see Dan giving his number to Nicky. We always joke about Dan's ability to secure a lady's number with his smooth talking and his self–proclaimed 'ironman body', but this brought a huge smile to my face. Over what actually must have looked like a dead body, he was managing to give out his number.

I woke from that treatment and felt completely

different. I felt rejuvenated and as though most of the tension had been removed from my legs. My Achilles were more relaxed and the soothed quads meant there was much less pressure on my knee joints – I was set for more miles on the bike. Nicky had done something to me besides treating my legs. In setting her healing hands on my troublesome areas, she had given me some invaluable peace of mind. With zero disrespect intended for the team, someone who knew exactly what they were doing had finally tended to my body and offered me a new sense of hope that it would survive the remaining miles. I took a huge smile away from that treatment room.

Walking, rather than hobbling back outside, I was greeted by the team who were ready and prepared with more food - McDonalds. Good work Will! Amid stuffing the second burger and chips into my face I was overjoyed to see a member of the Blazing Saddles RCC. The team are a collection of the finest cycling fanatics who get together throughout the year to partake in some of the best events that cycling has to offer. Phil Parsons was the team representative who came to meet me in Preston and it was a real pleasure to see him there chatting with all the others. I wanted to stop and chat to him about the adventure and perhaps sit down with a cup of tea and discuss the next places I would ride through. But following the treatment and the time taken away from my attempt, I was also super keen to get back on the saddle and put my 'new legs' to work.

I left that car park in Preston bound for more Southern climes with a contented feeling and a joy that I am still unable to describe. Receiving that lifeline could have perhaps saved the record attempt for it patched me up in so many ways. The impact of Nicky's work was all too evident to the team and I could hear many of them cheering and joking with a new found enthusiasm. We were having a second wind and the ride was getting back on track.

Wigan, Warrington, Whitchurch was my next set of towns to conquer. I knew once I'd reached Whitchurch that I would once again be greeted by Clive Middleton and Chris Wood who would be ready to ride alongside me and keep me going with all the stories on their cycling CV's. Dan was my company through the early part of the night and he kept using Whitchurch as the next major marker. With the others already there and waiting for me, I had to stay in the saddle and continue pedalling otherwise they'd be waiting there for nothing. Despite my rejuvenated state, I still had no idea what day it was and I didn't understand at all until the ride was over. Neither did I get a firm grasp of how many miles I had remaining. In fact, nothing seemed clear or easy to understand anymore.

I struggled through the major built up areas, using Dan as my guide for most of it. The fact that everywhere looked the same hampered my positive spirits, as I was unable to tell myself how we were making progress. Much like the lanes around Kilmarnock, these roads all looked the same; the buildings and junctions all alike. What I found disconcerting was how the streets were full of people dressed to the nines for a night on the town. Many were shouting comments about lycra and cycling. From what I remember, many of the people heckling were wearing more revealing clothing than my pair of lycra shorts.

There were, however, little offerings of encouragement from the road side through this part of England. At one of the morning's earlier hours, Dan and I were climbing a hill through Warrington when someone at the side of the road shouted cheerful praise. They shouted my name and wished me well for making it to Land's End. Now I had a pretty good view of the person but I had no idea who it was. I checked with Dan to see if, by any chance, it was somebody that he knew, but we continued riding, none the wiser. What a tremendous inspiration that was. It caused me to turn and face forward, determined to put more power through the pedals; the fact that a total stranger was there in the cold and dark to cheer me on, in a place that I'd never had anything to do with moved me. Shortly after this happened, I received several messages which had been posted on the website. The generous words of those people following were now helping to turn the pedals. I was reminded of Mark Solon's earlier messages, including those that told stories of followers bettering themselves as a result of my ride. It spurred further action and every turn of the pedals was indeed getting me closer to the finish.

The road south became very undulating and some of the climbs were a real struggle to get over. The effort I was putting in through this cold section was leading to a lot of soreness in my legs, particularly in my left calf, and my lungs were feeling heavy and blocked. I could feel the tension through the medial head of the calf muscle so I started pushing the pedal with my foot at an angle. While this solution offered a temporary rest from the original pain, I then caused more significant discomfort for my Achilles and my knee. Nothing was working in my favour.

The road became much wider and more open and I knew this meant I was back on the A49 level with North Wales. Although it wasn't a great distance between until the next arranged physio stop, it felt like an eternity before I finally made it there. I gave Dan an extremely hard time about this. The rain was coming down (so I was surprised that Dan was out on the bike) and the temperature was really dropping further. It wasn't a particularly pleasant night ride, but Dan had wanted to ride alongside me until we met his good friend, Clive. There happen to be a terrific number of roundabouts on the A49 and Dan kept telling me the physio and Clive would meet me at 'the next roundabout'. The next roundabout would arrive, and they wouldn't be there. Yet the rain would still be falling! The same was true at the next roundabout, the one after that, the one after that, and I am sure several more. Dan kept his cool and kept cycling beside me knowing that I was losing my tussle with tiredness. He knew I wanted to get to sleep but he kept me moving until such time as the van came into sight and I was able to hop off the bike. The promise of a physio session and warm food had kept me going for the past 66 miles. It finally arrived.

7.

"When you feel like giving up, remember why you held on so
long in the first place"
(Anonymous).

The ride had become quite an ordeal. It was a series of recurring problems that inevitably led to the loss of enjoyment (and isn't too easy to make exciting through writing!). Both the team and I were losing function from being so tired, and the monotony is hard to convey. A degrading, hungry body was turning the pedals, sometimes slowly, sometimes quickly, and sometimes barely at all while seven others sat motionless in the vehicles staring at this rather uneventful feat ahead of them. And we could so easily have adopted those thoughts. It would have been frightfully simple. But in those times of repeated struggles, and amongst all the hell of recurring dramas it was essential to remain focused on the original intentions. This was all just a part of the process in getting to the finish line.

Patrick (the acquired physiotherapist) set to work straight away on my legs. I was kept warm and dry (ish) under a huge pile of blankets and jackets while he worked vigorously on my various ailments. I was awake during this session unlike the one in Preston mainly because the rain was falling on my face. I was able to pay attention to what was going on this time and was shocked at how sore my joints were. I could feel the benefits of Patrick's work as he was doing it, and I looked forward to continuing with the added support of all the strapping that he was applying to my legs. I told myself that although everything inside my leg might be falling apart, this bright pink, very manly strapping would at least hold it together in the right place for me to keep using it. Quite a ridiculous thought I now think.

I rolled onto my back to get some treatment on my quads and lay there with my face being washed a little by the refreshing drizzle from the night sky. Jude, Clive's wife, was filling me up with cookies and chips that had clearly been bought a long time ago. They were now cold. I was left crunching through solid, crunchy chips, hoping they would help me recover and feel full of energy. They didn't.

Patrick's treatment was so good, I actually felt relaxed. I felt reassured having Jude and Clive's comments about my progress and also the encouragement from Clive to keep going. In truth I think they were surprised to see me again. I jumped into my rain coat and hopped back on the saddle.

At first I was fairly sprightly and I knew that Clive and Chris would be there riding beside me to keep me awake during the very midst of that cold, wet, gloomy night. I don't know whether they were expecting such a contrast from the previous ride we'd had northbound. The last time we'd ridden had been so much faster and we'd eaten away at the miles faster than a hungry hyena. This time however, I was riding more like the carcass that hyena was eating. I was barely moving the bike at all. The roads were completely abandoned, save the lorries that came hurtling along, towing their clouds of surface water at the perfect height for a cyclist to get soaked. I wonder what they must have thought, seeing a cyclist in the middle of this horrible night, cycling so slowly while a series of vehicles drove equally slowly right behind. Did they think I was mad? Did they think it was silly? Whatever they thought, they didn't slow down.

I was very relieved to have Chris and Clive either side of me, because I was fighting my biggest battle with extreme tiredness. My eyes fought to stay open, my brain failed to process much at all and I remember blurring my dreams with the actual events before me. This had to be the most significant toil with tiredness because sandwiched between these two giants on a bike I was falling asleep for upwards of 30 seconds at a time.

I was trying to hold sensible conversations with these guys – discussing anything and everything that happened to enter our heads. I had reached the point where I was unable to maintain 'polite small talk' so the topics had to be about something at least interesting otherwise I just shut off straight away. I knew I was tiring, but I didn't want to completely stop and take another rest: I was running too tightly to the schedule for my liking.

I awoke suddenly and turned to Chris on my

right. I tried to hide the fact that I had just dozed off, so I continued the conversation…. "I am sure there are some famous Welsh people". There was an extremely awkward silence and Chris just looked at me with a very blank face. I immediately felt very awake, and realised that what I'd just said in no way aligned with the conversation we had been having. Chris gave a very small, concerned smile and said "keep going mate, we're not that far now." Not that far?! Not that far from where? I was fairly certain that I still had a long way to go, but 'not that far' sounded like a good distance for me to have left. This ride was full of approximations!

I jerked aggressively as I woke again and this time I turned to Clive, fully aware that I had almost veered into him during that latest cat nap. I was also acutely aware of how slowly I was freewheeling and that my legs were stock-still! Clive, in his very broad accent simply said: "You'll get there a lot quicker if you pedal the bloody thing". Sound advice; he had a point.

I had to get something into my system to wake me up. Several of my support crew were, by now, as high as a kite on Red Bull. Nobody more so than Ben. I discussed the idea between me and myself for a matter of minutes before requesting that I got something warm inside my stomach and also a Red Bull shot. I could see the shock on several faces at my request, but seeing any form of expression on Ben's face was tough given the permanent wide eyed grin the Red Bull had forced his face to display.

I put to one side how much I hated the taste of this product, but thought I would risk it if it would keep me awake and my hopes of reaching Land's End alive. I downed a quick cup of tea that at least made me feel human. (I think tea is the most amazing drink. Regardless of what has happened, tea seems to possess a mystery 'something' that makes everything seem ok. It also offers a sense of clarity and makes even the most demoralising task seem better). I chased the cup of tea with one of these small Red Bull shots that I know are not great for the body. But I swallowed the sweet, pungent smelling liquid and hoped that it would keep me functioning.

Back on the road, moving at a better pace for at least ten minutes, my eyelids were stuck wide open, the potent Red Bull fighting my urge even to blink. My brain was trying to establish a way of sleeping with my eyes this wide open, and my legs were caught in the crossfire between my sleepy brain, and my overly open eyelids. It would have been more amusing if my legs had decided to split loyalties at this stage where one continued cycling and the other refused altogether. But this didn't happen. They simply both decided to give up at the same time. I don't blame them. Had the road been downhill, this wouldn't have been such an issue, but given the undulations in the route, this caused quite a considerable problem. Particularly when, ten minutes later, my eyelids also decided that they'd had enough. Not only had they had enough, but following their dramatic high, they took their dramatic low. My eyelids were clamped together, tighter than a nun's thighs, and there seemed to be nothing that would open them up. I was increasingly aware that the mile count down had almost ground to a halt and those around me made me aware of this painfully slow pace. On the occasions when I would reach an incline, I thought the countdown would actually start to count up again.

I felt surges of energy in my body and would turn the pedals hard for several revolutions, increasing my pace to an electrifying 15 mph perhaps, which at the time felt like I was leading a huge race. I would soon fall back and be slumped in my saddle acutely aware of my struggle. The glances and the anxious looks shared between the support crew and those riding beside me spoke volumes. I was desperately failing to cover the miles.

The night sky eventually changed to a lighter blue. The shades of the clouds lightened and the horizon and the road side became silhouetted against what would become a morning sky. Clive used this as my target to ride into the morning and to try and make that my last night of riding before Land's End. I liked the sound of that, and it made the finish seem touchable. Was I really approaching my last day of riding before it would all be over? Could it be that I was that close to finishing the ride later that day?

No. But it sounded encouraging.

Clive and Chris helped me drag my sorry self to

Ludlow where I met the motor home parked in a layby. I was soaked through and had nothing, absolutely nothing left to give. The team was all too aware of the battle I'd been through during the course of that night, and so it was decided that I would be given a long sleep to try and make the final push more manageable. It was here that I was given an hour of uninterrupted sleep, properly tucked up in one of the beds at the back of the motor home, carefully tucked in by Tony who made sure every single need I might have had was met.

I awoke confused and surprised, but overjoyed, to see a very familiar face. Matt Hartley, a friend from home stood beside my bed. He greeted me with a big smile and a hug. It was wonderful to see him, and it took me a few moments to put together what he was doing there.

He'd come all the way up from Cardiff to cycle with me! He'd taken the train to Hereford and then cycled 24miles along the route to meet us in Ludlow. What a hero. It was so good to see him, and it was a magnificent time to see another familiar face. He was full of encouragement and jumped on his bike to ride along behind.

I loved knowing he was there with me, but I felt bad seeing him wearing a jumper and a 'normal' pair of shorts. I tried to offer him some of my kit, but he refused to take any of it. Perhaps the team had mentioned to him what had happened in most of that kit, or perhaps he was just sharp enough to work out for himself that it would not be the cleanest of clothing to put on. I chatted as much I could to Matt while trying to ease my knee back into the movement of cycling again. It had really seized up during that sleep. I found it very difficult to allow my knee to relax and this made my cycling action very awkward. I was poking at the pedals and not transferring much power. The discomfort in my knee at the time I can barely describe. It was almost like holding a brand new chalk against the chalk board and rolling those crisp sharp edges against the board until such time as the pressure and grinding movement causes the chalk to crumble and break away, rounding off the edges into a smooth tip. If my knee was the chalk, that is what it felt like.

Mentally, however, I felt like a new person following that long sleep, but my entire body had seriously stiffened in the time that I'd been counting sheep. I regretted the sleep for that pain in my knees, but I knew that it had helped immeasurably for my mind, and that was now my main weapon for completing this ride. I was impressed beyond all suitable adjectives at how long Matt cycled with me. Having only completed a small number of rides previously, he rode 24 miles to where he joined me and then rode the next 170 miles of my route! Having this new company, but also having the mental rest proved to have been essential to the attainment of a positive mood. I had been berating myself for feeling useless, something that only served to act as a downward spiral. Not a downward helix I was later informed by Tony, because then the bad patches would remain at the same frequency. It was a spiral, because the frequency of these really bad episodes was increasing. I was still going round and round regardless!

Pete once told me that a physical challenge is only 50% physical, 40% mental, and then the last 10% is in the heart. I thought about these sentiments a great deal. On that basis I had done the physical content of the ride. I was now firmly into the mental stage of the ride and to that end I knew I had to use my mind-tools and stubbornness to over-ride any of the bodily issues that I was experiencing. I had to find that 'mental strength' that so many people talk about in endurance sports, but where was I going to find it? I had to first find it in the ignorance of my knee. I took a deep breath, holding it at the deepest part, and then released that air at the same time as relaxing my leg. Despite the first burst of pain, my knee was back riding in smooth, even circles.

I turned to the thoughts of home and found a

great deal more strength in the messages that people were sending to the team. Particularly as I was getting closer to the Westcountry I felt more and more intense emotions as a result of the encouragement. More and more frequently this emotion would boil over into a few tears, but for many other times I had nothing but a huge grin on my face. Pete remembers that I mainly wore a painful expression, shown best through my eyes as I stared at the front wheel of my bike, so perhaps that smile was also in my mind. I enjoyed moments when a leaf would stick to my tyre and I would have something to take my mind away from the monotony of the road. Its constant return gave me something to look forward to and I was disappointed when it would fall off.

It had been raining most of the previous night while riding with Clive and Chris and the roads bore the evidence; wide puddles and water filled pot holes again. In my non-observant state of mind I managed to find many of these holes, and it only served to make the progress that little less comfortable. I was riding with Tony beside me, and we'd reduced our conversations to very short, almost instructional interaction. I was cognisant of how the episodes near Glasgow when I lost my mental functioning were still causing a great deal of concern for Tony, and his primary focus was ensuring my survival to Land's End, but something had changed and we no longer had the jovial banter-filled conversations that we so often partake in while on the saddle together and I missed that. I was acutely aware of how tired my support riders must have been also – they were putting in some big miles between them, and they too were surviving on less than normal levels of sleep, coupled with the responsibility of looking after this nutcase on the bike.

I started living in my own world, and although I felt bad about not talking to Matt who had come all that way to ride with me, I felt a sense of security about that little world I retreated to. I didn't want to acknowledge my pains to anybody anymore. I needed that other person in my head to complain to; only they would be able to help me, I could no longer manage it myself. I had had what I thought was my final physio treatment, and so I was preparing myself to haul my increasingly useless bulk through the rest of South Wales and then through the entire Westcountry. This was not something that I looked forward to, but I knew with the right frame of mind I would be able to overcome the pain that I was experiencing. I kept telling myself that the pain would soon be gone; that I would receive some medical help and they would be able to patch me up with whatever was necessary. I clung to the hope that after a good sleep I would feel much better. And with that thought I imagined cold pillows and warm beds, a soft feather duvet that I could wrap myself into while the light from a window filled the room all around me. I had to push these thoughts out – they only served to make me more tired, and as my brain indulged itself in these thoughts of slowing down for a rest, my performance was matching it. I had to think of something more lively, more energetic. After all, I (hopefully) had less than 20 hours of cycling and it would all be over.

Matt, Tony and I continued through the route, dodging the growing traffic. The road surface was pretty terrible and there were often sharp, challenging ascents on which I tired to maintain my pace. Although I was pushing my body to ride up with the required average, I was acutely aware of the added damage that I was causing to my legs. "You've got less than 20 hours to go now…they'll last that long at least" I kept telling myself. I think this was more hope than fact.

It was at the start of one of those climbs when I had a boost from a fellow member of the ultra cycling community. Ann Woolridge who had been leaving countless messages of support was positioned at the side of the road with her iconic 'WolfSpider' decorated van. It was quite a shock to suddenly see her appear on the route, but it was the scattered start of some tremendous roadside support for the remainder of the journey. The red tracking dot on the website had thoroughly established a firm following, with many more people now hitting their refresh buttons to keep checks on the team's progress. What that meant for the road side support was an up to date means by which they could position themselves ahead of the team. I have listened to numerous entertaining stories of people clicking refresh on their computer, jumping in the car, racing ahead to a known place on the route, and then driving back and forth the route frantically in order to find us! Every person who made it out to cheer, toot their horn, jump up and down or just point and grin, really had a significant impact.

As the day was starting to grow I became more and more aware of what lay ahead. I voiced my concern to several members of the team that there was still a demanding section ahead and that I would need plenty of support to get me through it. There was quite a navigational struggle getting through Monmouth. The Monmouth show was taking place, which brought many of the roads to a stand still. A source of local knowledge had convinced the trailing support van to guide me in a different direction than planned and this, combined with the heavy traffic resulted in the separation of myself and the team in an area of which I had no recollection or knowledge. I was now blindly following a man on a bike – something lots of other people had been doing since I'd started!

This situation caused a lot of tension among the team. The failings of my body, the tiredness of the team, and the pressures of completing the ride on schedule were all mounting to a powerful climax. But there was still a long way to go and we needed to remember that. There was no point in losing our tempers and getting angry when we were still so far from the end. That man I was blindly following made a great decision – he sent us on a route which helped us make it through the chaos and get back together much quicker. Leaving the pre-planned route was a decision made under extreme pressure, but the sharp thinking of Tom and Pete to embrace this contingency really paid off.

Eventually I made it through the network of roads, unaware of the full extent of the tension the traffic situation had caused. I spotted the motor home parked up ahead at the side of the road and made a real effort to get there as soon as I could. I was too tired to unclip my feet and wasn't that interested in stopping for long, so I lent up against the side of the van and put my hand through the window, hoping for a bit of contact, some food or something else. It was then that I was given a real lifeline – a lifeline that I knew would help guarantee the completion of the ride. It was Chloe.

I had so desperately wanted her there from the start. I had been through so much pain as a result of not having a physio, but none of that mattered now. I had a physical aid in which I had so much trust, but I also had a mental aid. Just her presence would carry me to the finish. She grabbed my hand from inside the van. I was over the moon and raced inside the van at my fastest hobble speed for an energy-filling hug. I was delighted to see her. I didn't know at the time, but my parents were also very close by, having driven miles to collect Chloe and then drop her with the team. I think at that moment it was best I didn't see them – I am sure I would have used their comfort as a means to break down. However, that time was one of being built up, and I enjoyed a quick snack and a 'comfort break' in the motor home before moving on out to the bike.

Knowing I had Chloe there enabled me to ride much more relaxed, I had already explained to her all my problems, and with absolute confidence she said she would be able to patch me up and keep me working. The team had planned a break in Aust services, just over the old Severn Bridge. I 'raced' through the rest of South Wales, joined by more friends on their bikes. Some people joined for a handful of miles, others joined for much longer. Matt Hartley was still riding! The last tough climb I remember was broken up by moments of madness provided by Richard Sambrook. I knew I was holding up a lot of traffic on the narrow roads, but thankfully I wasn't receiving too much abuse. None that I was aware of anyhow. One car came hurtling past with the driver leaning out the window screaming at the top of his voice. I turned to Hartley and asked in a very happy and very shocked voice: "Was that Sandy?!" Matt just grinned…it sure was. A little further up the road he appeared again, this time out of his car, dancing and singing at the side of the road. What a hero.

The mood really became more positive as Wales was drawing to a close. The team was laughing more, I was surrounded by extremely positive people and there was a sense of impending completion. But had it all come too soon? The roads felt full of excitement. I believe we can find a great deal of strength and support inside ourselves simply by searching for and understanding our own motivations, but to have the kind of friendship, and stranger support, that I was receiving helped my internal search beyond belief. Every message, every comment on the website, every cheer from the following supporters turned the pedals. I was soon going to be in the Westcountry.

Following the winding Wye Valley and seeing the signs for Chepstow added more fuel to the fire. Tony and I recalled riding through in the pouring night time rain just a few days ago and joked about the events which had happened between.

It confirmed that I had no perception of time any more and that I had no perception of what I was really doing. Time had simply become numbers, and days had become something so confusing I couldn't really follow, despite my craving to understand. We spotted another group of cyclists just before the Severn Bridge, all clad in orange jerseys, and with a bit of off road action we were soon on the cycle path behind them. I was keen to chase them down, unsure of the reason, but I wanted to catch them and know I was making progress. We crossed the bridge and headed in to the services, and what a service station stop it was.

All ready and waiting was Chloe with her massage table, set to patch my legs up further; her eager hands which I was all too aware were capable of inflicting serious pain 'for the greater good'. I jumped onto the massage table and longed for some sleep, but I was too excited and too much in pain to get any sleep at all. My parents were there at the services and it was wonderful to see them. I wanted to tell them all about what had been happening. I wanted to tell them how broken I was, but at the same time, I wanted to try and show my Mum that I'd recovered from my breakdown near Lancaster. The worry on her face when I first pulled up in the services was unbearable. I didn't like it and it looked doubtful. That car park was where I'd seen my parents for the last time on the northbound journey, so seeing them again felt almost like a confirmation that I was near the end (which I wasn't really!).

Paul DeLancey was also there, and I remember seeing him because of the extensive grin that he had on his face. Paul accompanied me as my support crew when I cycled across the USA in 2008. Seeing him there made me smile and filled me with many good memories. There was also an assortment of people from Bath and beyond who had taken 'extended lunch breaks' in order to come and show their support. Seeing them there and getting to shake their hands made me smile. These were people I didn't know that well which made it even more striking that they were there to support. I had always imagined it would just be my parents who would be interested in my progress, so learning about the magnitude of the following really shocked me. It was hard to comprehend that over 10 000 people were logging on to check my progress.

Having been fed a takeaway meal of burger and chips, and having washed that down with a banana smoothie, I was set to take on the Westcountry. The team was also getting excited and they were looking forward to getting the ride completed – mainly for the sake of getting home and having a proper sleep themselves! Will and I set out together with enough local knowledge to get ourselves well and truly on route. In fact I was still able to picture the entire remaining route – to Penzance at least.

Setting out from Aust services at quite some speed, I was eager to try and make Land's End before the break of the morning. I was aware that we would be extremely tight, and I knew my pace was slowing further, so I was delighted with the presence of some speed, albeit temporarily. I was more delighted to still have Matt Hartley riding with me and getting to talk to him was a real pleasure. We pressed on through Bristol, taking in the sight of the Clifton Suspension Bridge. I took that moment to eat and enjoy a packet of jelly. Simple pleasures (and sugars).

I was making good use of the bus lanes to avoid the building traffic as we got nearer and nearer to the centre. Thankfully there were no mishaps, and before long many supporters were meeting me on route. Pete's brother, Mike Scull, started the trend, and seeing him at the side of the road simply to cheer lightened the burden of the task. We started to gather more riders and by the time I was out on the A38 I had maybe 20 riders all offering support. We remained on the A38 taking in the sharp climbs and descents of the Mendip Hills. I would have enjoyed avoiding these, but I figured I was in the South West – I might as well get used to continual climbing. With plenty to keep my mind occupied I was able to push aside any thoughts of pain and discomfort. I used the growing group of cyclists behind me to focus on what I needed to do. My pedals were turning much easier with all that support, and I felt as though their willing for me to complete it pushed me up even the steepest of the hills. I was keen to keep an open road, however, and I became nervous when the group closed in too near to me. Less nervous from worry of their riding, more nervous because I knew how unstable I had become and how terribly slow my reactions now were.

I had a food bag of cookies in my jersey pocket

that I was keen to get opened and into my body. By this stage, Dan had jumped out and had joined Will and I on the bikes, and I was also reassured to see Russ Coles again. Amid the busyness of the growing group, people joining all the time, I was relieved to have the protection and the calming influence of Will, Dan and Russ. They helped get the food into me, and also helped maintain my focus, pointing out the people and the supporters that I might have missed from my introverted state.

There was one supporter who I would never have missed, however. Following in her car, with her mother at her side, Sharon Cox, a secondary school teacher of mine, blasted the horn and then screamed out the window. At first I was convinced by the sound of the horn that I had one highly strung driver behind who had perhaps struggled to get past. Yet, as the car pulled level and again sounded the horn with a long, continuous blast, I turned to see Sharon screaming support. That was in Highbridge. All the way to Taunton she leapfrogged the group making sure every time more encouragement was delivered. What a hero – it didn't just lift my spirits and make me laugh, but it lifted everybody's.

A group of twenty-five or so riders joined me to Bridgwater and then Taunton. The supporting crowds that were gathering at the side of the road were way above what I had expected and I was starting to see faces that I hadn't for so long. What a way to gain encouragement than from seeing family, friends, friends of friends and even strangers lining the streets and cheering. I often wonder what they thought as I went past – the more honest people among them tell me that I looked like a zombie and that my eyes were vacant despite any hint of a smile. Others try to tell me that I was looking strong. Looking strong?!

I was once running a marathon and had completely run out of energy as a result of poor fluid intake. I started struggling from the 22-mile mark and by the time I eventually reached the 24 mile mark, I was doubting whether I would ever make it through the last couple of miles without wheelchair assistance and someone to push. I was barely moving, struggling to place one foot in front the other. I passed a marshal, no other runners around me. He stood up from his chair, clapping and cheering, and then said, "you look so strong. You're almost there. Great performance!" I was unsure. I knew I was barely moving, I felt like I was barely moving, and I remember my face hiding not a bit of the pain and frustration that I was feeling. I appreciate the encouragement, but as a strong realist, I much preferred the marshal's comments at mile 25. "Just over a mile and then all the pain will stop." Much better.

My parent's house lies just off the route near Taunton and I was keen to see how I would feel heading past there and not stopping. I was glad it was still daylight as I felt darkness would make me want to curl up inside and simply dream about the last 160 miles. But dreaming

by day and making the dreams reality is what I opted for –
or, being totally honest, what Will forced me to do! I
suggested to him that I get one last sleep at Taunton before
making the very final push to Land's End. What better
place than my own bed where I would be comfortable and
could eat all the proper food I wanted? Well Will decided
that was the worst possible option, refusing to even let me
talk about it anymore. He said: "you can stop somewhere
else, but not here!"

So I passed through Taunton unable to decipher
what most people were saying, but from their liveliness
and the amazing banners, I felt a wave of goose-bumps
across my body. I clocked several faces and tried to wave,
but for the most part I was numb to the fact that there

were individuals.
Their collective force
propelled me along
the road, but I
couldn't take in every
face – I guess I never
could anyway.

Leaving Taunton, still
on the A38, I knew I
was bound for
Wellington. But after
the uplift of passing
through Taunton, I felt

the potential effects of a come down. I started to feel very tired and my knees were causing a lot more pain. I have since likened the boost from all the support to taking the Red Bull back in the Midlands. It gave me a tremendous lift, helping me find energy and motivation, but once it was removed, I felt a slump. It was therefore a most welcome discovery to realise that all along the route until the end there were supporters to keep topping up the levels of energy. Regardless, I needed to sleep otherwise I would have fallen off my bike.

The team set up camp in Waitrose, Wellington and told me I could have some hot food. I took the rest time to get some treatment from Chloe who helped my legs relax. I stuffed the hot fish and chips down, feeling their warmth and hoping it would remain until the end. I was chatting to the entire team who were reassuring me of my progress and projecting finish times. The website and the mobile went crazy with messages during this stop with people up in arms about why I had stopped. I had to!! I was sad at this stage to lose Matt Hartley who had cycled all the way from Ludlow. This was the longest ride that Matt had completed by an absolutely huge margin and he was still going strong. He had wanted to make it all the way to the end of the ride, but owing to his ability to hold down a respectable job he was forced to head back. But what a tremendous effort to make it from Ludlow to Wellington. It was a pleasure to have him on the saddle beside me and I wish he could have stayed longer.

After a very short snooze I was woken and put back on the bike. There were still a good number of people who had stayed around to ride with me, despite my poorly timed sleep, and I smiled greatly at the thought of having company. However, I was also concerned about progress and wanted to make sure that I wouldn't come a cropper with so few miles remaining. The group and I headed out of Wellington and for the Devon border. I was keen to get into the fast, well-surfaced section of the Exe Valley, so I wanted to make sure we gained the miles at a reasonable speed. I was still confident I knew the route very well and I knew I could ride it quickly, so flanked by those very close friends I made my way into Devon. We exited the A361 at Tiverton and duly followed the winding, rural Exe Valley road towards Bickleigh, and then ultimately Exeter which the team were using as my next target. Then I would be on my final road – the notorious A30. How would I deal with the A30 when that was all that stood between me and Land's End? Would I make it over the hills?!

But I still had the Exe Valley to go at this point. I was riding tightly with Will, but also getting plenty opportunity to chat with Matt Morgan, Paddy Goodall, Ben Harvey and Owen Thomas – four people I was delighted to have on the saddle around me. I enjoyed sharing stories of the ride with them, and they helped me keep a decent pace through scenery that is best enjoyed at a leisurely pace. (It was a leisurely pace if you ask Ben!).

Ordinarily I would sit back in the saddle and enjoy the view of the valley, the tranquillity of the fields beside the road, but there was no time for this, and darkness was already descending. I was sad to lose these guys when we arrived at Exeter, but I imagined a final push to the end would require some serious focus. Being able to chat to these friends distracted me from the severe aches and pains, so once they were gone I was left to fester in my own moans and worries.

Passing through Exeter happened like a dream and doing it all with Will as my main navigator from the saddle we passed through with utmost ease. I was joined by Simon Williams who was hiding behind a lamp post somewhere along the road, and he jumped out and joined in with the group's pace perfectly. It was a wonderful, wonderful surprise to see Simon. He brought yet another fresh sense of conversation and I was keen to get talking to him about what had been happening. Simon and I had completed numerous rides together during my training and so he was a very familiar person to ride with. We'd struggled and suffered in training with each other, so I knew he would be able to ride sympathetically with me. There were just over 120 miles remaining and I was hoping he would sit with me until the very end.

As we progressed on the A30 I became immeasurably frustrated with the lack of visible progress. I lost control of my cycling and allowed my frustrations to take over. The difficulty was riding an open road with nothing to put the speed or the gradient into perspective. The cat-eyes and the central barrier continued regardless of the speed and I resented the horizon for giving zero indication of how I was progressing. The only guide that I could offer myself was my cadence but this was so erratic that it really offered nothing constructive. I kept asking those around me for my current speed, and I am certain that they were telling huge fibs. They'd say I was riding at 14mph when I knew it was much slower. I was struggling to remain balanced at times, my cadence down to as little as 40 or 50 revolutions per minute.

From this debacle, Tony's report states: "My initial conversations with Ben when I rejoined him on the saddle were a little awkward. Over the previous night rides I had become accustomed to treating him almost like a child. This was what proved appropriate on those occasions, when I had to constantly remind him to eat and drink, and also had to keep a very close watch on his level of tiredness using a "sleepiness" scale of 1 to 10! However for whatever reason he now appeared to have a newfound clarity of thought and was not very appreciative of what I think he perceived as condescending reminders to eat and drink, never mind my regular questions about his tiredness! On one occasion upon asking him to rate his level of tiredness he challenged me to elaborate on the rationale of my scale and its usefulness. To be honest I had no idea what he was talking about at the time and was more preoccupied with astonishment by his apparent lucidness! He later responded, only to query my level of tiredness, again wondering which scale I in turn was going to use to answer his question!"

Anyone who has driven or cycled the A30 knows that it seems to go on and on forever. The hills seem to grow before you, and as soon as you reach the top of one, you can see ahead to the next climb in your path. The main difference at night: You don't get to see what lies ahead. You don't even get to see if you're on a climb or a descent. The cat-eyes indicate nothing, other than the same line you've been looking at for the past however many miles. The central barrier occasionally changes shape to make you aware that you are in actual fact moving, but it is far from convincing. I mean the miles on the signs were decreasing so slowly, but I felt like I was on a gym bike and not actually making any progress. I gained more pleasure from being on my rollers in my dark bedroom, staring at a flickering candle light. I tried to remember those training sessions where I'd ride the length of a five-inch candle whilst on the rollers. They lasted for hours and hours and I wished for something to melt the candle faster. Nothing helped, sadly. This time on the A30 was comparable to a candle that was growing in length. It was at best, failing to melt and I was failing to maintain hope.

I also tried to liken the situation to the 'roundabout rides' that I'd completed in the early stages of my training. In my hometown there is a stretch of dual carriageway just over a mile in length with a roundabout at either end. To gain some sort of insight to how I dealt with boredom I cycled for ten hours between those roundabouts through the night. There was nothing to see, no scenery change at all, and very few vehicles on the road for me to pay attention to. I was confined to the world of my front wheel. Somehow I managed to survive that night and in completing 240 miles without any stimulation I learned to operate an internal world where I was able to satisfy my mind in the complete absence of stimulation. But I had seemingly forgotten this by now – I was unable to get away from the desperate feeling of frustration.

I allowed that emotion to deepen. It was nagging at me intensely, preventing me from thinking straight and creating a whirlwind of anxiety and confusion in my mind. My eyes were unable to focus properly and all around me were white lights, red lights, flashing orange lights, reflective clothing. It was a world of vibrancy in front of me and it dazzled all the thoughts I could muster. The monotony of the task was wearing me down, spinning me mentally as though I were in a washing machine. This then lead to a rapid deterioration in my feelings and performance. Everything seemed out of my control and I was not comfortable with that. I wanted to be in charge of something that was happening to me; I had to do something for myself, and so I requested a sleep. I was struggling to maintain open eyes, and on a road such as the A30, it is important to be awake; even in these late hours of the night / early hours of the morning. I was granted five minutes sleep and a donut, at the end of which I was woken rather unconventionally by the team playing music as loud as possible. I was pushed back onto the bike, being told with no uncertainty that that was to be my very final stop. This was it then: The very last effort before making it to Land's End.

Cars were flying past (so I recall), beeping horns, shouting out the window, and playing music at maximum volume. Cars were filling the laybys, still beeping their horns, shouting further encouragement from their windows, while some drivers stood out on the roadside, cheering with utmost enthusiasm. I couldn't believe they were so full of energy. This was a time of pain and unhappiness. What were they thinking?! Many of the road bridges had banners hanging down from them, and in one case there was a Police car with flashing blue lights and my (unmet at the time) relatives shouting at the top of their voices. The Police had stopped to enquire what they were all doing, gathered atop the bridge in the middle of the night. Once they'd explained, the officer joined the troop of supporters, lending his blue lights as encouragement. In turn that Police car came whizzing by – the officer leaning over the passenger seat to shout encouragement from out his window. I knew several of us were not displaying correct lights, or even had lights, and we were hardly riding close to the edge and in single or dual file as we should; we were all over the carriageway. Imagine being fixed up now for not having lights!

All the missed sleep had created significant troubles, but amid the excitement of the impending finish it was soon too much for me to handle. The effects of the tiredness and the failing of my body took its toll. As Tony said, we shared conversations about vertices, sliding scales and the validity of a communal sleepiness scale. That's right, we were attempting to rate each other's sense of tiredness on a scale. Perhaps it was my dislike for this scale that made me feel anxious, but Tony tells me that I was quite defensive, trying to pin the tiredness on those around me! The rest of the team in the vehicles also tell of my further strange behaviours. I started to encourage the blasting of the horn, using my arm in much the same way that I still, at 24 years of age, try to make lorry drivers sound their horn. The team responded and I repeatedly did this with great enthusiasm. I only recall doing it a couple of times, but according to them it went on for many miles!

I sprinted after the van, trying to catch the camera that was being dangled out the window. Before long I slumped back into my snail-like pace, complaining about the bits of my body that were no longer working. My behaviour and emotions were bouncing like a yo-yo. I was really keen to share the pot of Lindt truffles that my Mum had given. I am a gigantic Lindt fan, so when they were handed out of the van, that simple treat heavily excited me. The only problem – they were wrapped and I could no longer control my hands. I had to enlist the help of those around me to un-wrap them and hand them back to me. Sadly one truffle fell during the transfer process.

I struggled further with the monotony of the A30. Little episodes of interaction were vital for breaking it up so I was honoured with the efforts that were being made by Tony and Simon. I struggled with the same actions bringing the same responses: the same white line, or another cat's eye. Nothing changed. Nothing at all. Not even the skyline. Nothing remotely changed. I was getting frustrated and was paying ever-increasing attention to my ailments. I was constantly complaining about them and at times I perceived the encouragement to ride a little faster as serious insensitivity concerning my pain. It was far from a case of insensitivity. It was exactly what I needed to get the ride over with.

I wondered how long until I might feel my hands again, or when my feet might start to gain sensations. I thought about bursting my legs to drain all the fluid away and how long it would take to get my nether regions back to life and under control again. I hadn't been able to locate my testicles for over 72 hours and the numbness that had engulfed my midriff worried me. My voice and my mouth were aspects I was keen to get back, for the principle reason that I didn't want to have to fill my mouth with strepsils for several minutes before eating solid foods. And because of that pain I had by now given up eating. It was a major, mountainous battle for Tony to try and get me to eat and drink. I was refusing to consume anything, which was only detrimental to my performance. I couldn't see beyond my stubbornness, so I persisted in my refusal. Everything was going wrong. I may have had only a few miles remaining and many hours to complete them, but I lacked the composure and the attitude to make it to the end.

I don't know why, but with 50 miles still to go, I started to wind down. I had been joined by one of the lecturers from my undergrad who engaged me in more conversations. He also used the sleepiness scale to monitor my downward spiral of tiredness which I am sure was leading to conversations between everyone around me. I was just too vacant of mind to realise what they were discussing. Dan was sent out from the motor home to try and talk some sense into me and to keep me working, but even he had one heck of a struggle. I had almost given up. The A30 was beating me and I was beating myself. Simon and I had exhausted our list of famous Welsh people. We'd combined our new list with that which I started alongside Clive Middleton. I was feeling quite proud of it by the time Simon and I had finished up – we had a list of five!

By starting to wind down my mind and body felt as though they had pretty much finished this gruelling ride. This angers me to look back at my attitude at that point, because I hadn't finished it until such time as I'd arrived at Land's End. There were no half measures in this ride. The finish line is called the finish line for a reason. I slowed considerably and I relied wholly on the determination of those beside me just to keep the pedals going round at whatever pace they could convince my legs to move.

Finally my stubbornness relented. I piled into the motor home and begged for a donut. I stuffed it in and then started with the cookies and the chocolates. Then I began my deep and meaningful plea to the team. They were sat in front of me, some at the table, some stood in the doorway; others more comfortably sprawled out in the crow's nest bed. I explained to them how I was now in a very desperate place; franticly searching for their help and that I would need all their skills to get to the end. I was pouring my heart out to them, letting them know that I could no longer function on my own. I needed help.

By this moment on the route, Ben must have been defying altitude sickness. He was now higher than a kite on red bull – constantly topping himself up to prevent the awful crashes that it was bringing to the team – cyclists and drivers alike. He was shaking from the effects of it and had been behind the wheel of that motor home for the previous 30 hours straight. That has to be a serious record in itself?! Clearly he was excited about the finish, I think because he knew he would finally be able to relax. He wasn't keen on me having been stopped for so long, so following my rallying cries to the team, trying to recruit support and atmosphere he said what was on his mind. In the broadest possible Somerset accent, Ben yelled: "Get on ye lazy sod." Say no more; I was out the van.

I clocked a road sign that said Penzance – 20 miles, which even in my completely ruined state told me that I was near Redruth. I'd spent so long training on this road, that I knew the mileages. I just didn't know the road so well in the dark. Sensing Penzance so close and what, on a fresh day, is a one-hour ride I wanted to try and increase the speed. I managed for a couple of miles before the pain in my legs and the lack of reserves in my body decided otherwise. I went back to spinning the pedals, and looking helplessly at Dan. His small smile let me know that the end was near and that he felt I was definitely going to make it. I now knew I could certainly get there ahead of the existing record, but what I hadn't told everyone apart from my sponsors was that I believed I could do it in less than 6 days. I had only a matter of hours left to keep my word.

There was a great atmosphere that ebbed and flowed through the team. There was the impending finish which seemed within touching distance every time a little more effort was put through the pedals. But every time this happened, the pain became too much to tolerate and the atmosphere would decline just as fast as it had built. Tony mustered as much as he could, using strong cheers to pick me up. Most often they would work, but only as temporary fixes. We continued with the goal of beating sunrise to Land's End.

Penzance arrived not a moment too soon. My parents and my neighbour, Gary Chaplin, who were there by the roadside report how the four of us on the bikes and the support vans passed them at a snail's pace in total, utter silence. They sensed the desperation in the air and ceased their cheering and clapping, opting instead to look on at what resembled a funeral procession. I do not recall seeing them, and to that end, they have said that nobody from saddle or van gave their presence any acknowledgement. Despite being so close, they questioned whether I would make it to the end.

Someone, however, made the decision that enough was enough. Land's End had to be close, so what did it matter if in these final stages I left body parts strewn along the road. I had had enough and I wanted to get off this bike. The atmosphere among the four of us felt as though it had suddenly been plugged in. There were a few moments of growing anticipation, a few sideways glances and a series of small, wry smiles shared between us before the explosion finally took place. I stepped on the pedals and gritted my teeth. I knew these riders around me were about to take me into a whole new world of pain, far beyond anything I had already experienced.

Dan, Tony and Simon shouted their excitement as the pace increased; their shouts gaining decibels with every mile an hour. We were racing along, refusing to decrease speed for corner or climb – however difficult it might be. It was electrifying. It might sound ridiculous at the end of almost 1900 miles, but the gears all shifted, the cadence went through the roof, the pain scales were unable to register and the pace increased to 30 mph. There were still plenty of climbs, some much sharper than I'd remembered, with several tight corners thrown in the mix, but none of these hampered the speed. There seemed to be more energy summoned with every hair that stood on the back of my neck, and the growing number of goose-bumps over my body was matched with the growing anticipation of reaching the line.

My body was experiencing more pain than it had ever felt before. My injured body parts were screaming at the grotesque force that I was asking them to produce. My energy systems were complaining profusely about how much I suddenly demanded from them and my lungs and heart felt unsure whether they would even attempt to meet the demands I was placing on them. I was concerned for how much farther it would be to the end – I had been expecting it already. Where had it gone? I didn't want an anti-climax now. I had started the fastest ten-mile time trial of my life and I couldn't ease up yet. We went sailing past my parents' car. They'd pulled in near the top of a climb hoping to offer some words of encouragement to spur me on to the finish. As we flew past the vehicle, still at 30mph and attempting to shake off the support van, they stepped on the accelerator to race us into Land's End.

Amid the heavy breathing and strained voices that were groaning under the extreme energy outputs, Simon's chain jumped. In a split second I questioned whether we ought to stop or carry on. My legs wouldn't allow me to stop and then get back to that level of pain. Fortunately with half a second more and before I'd reached any decisive conclusion, Simon had got it back on without having to stop. On we pressed, instantly back to the intense pace. Tony was screaming encouragement and it was echoed by Simon and Dan. I would dearly have loved to join in, but I had nothing to offer in any way – everything I was capable of doing was going through the pedals at that moment.

There was a very aggressive climb just further on when Dan's bike made a terrible sound; a sound just like the chain snapping. Fortunately his lousy gear change was all there was to blame so he was able to get it back without stopping, too. As pedals came close to tarmac, some actually touching, and as breathing became more and more laboured, the arrowhead that we'd created cut through the pre-dawn air and I rounded the final corner before Land's End. I saw the Land's End complex ahead of me in the very first of the morning's light. I didn't know what to make of it. It had been so long in coming, but it was now there within sight and it felt like I was cycling faster than I had ever cycled before. I could feel the emotions spilling over already and I struggled to intake enough breath to keep my legs turning. The immense pain that filled my body suddenly felt peaceful and I clung to that pain as I saw before me the finish line I'd been dreaming about for so very long. The continual flashing of camera lights filled the space in front of me. The finish line was right before me and there was no longer any reason why I couldn't cross it. I climbed out the saddle to make the final meters along the driveway and to once more feel the power of my body moving the bike that had carried me so far. I sailed through the line, fully on my brakes but still disappeared under the archway and into the Land's End complex before I finally came to a stop. I had made it! I had crossed the line. It was over.

While the charged emotions of crossing the line robbed me of the visual clarity I would have liked, finally getting to unclip from the pedals and have the bike taken away was the most wonderful feeling. I was engulfed by the team that had made the ride a success and together we had an ecstatic hug as we embraced each other and the over-spilling emotions. I was back at Land's End! Five days, twenty-one hours and eight minutes later.

8.

"Cycling is like a church. Many attend, but few
understand…You have just built a cathedral."
(D. Badger)

The team and I, along with family and friends, enjoyed the new light of the morning as we toasted everyone's efforts with a bottle of champagne and discussed numerous events throughout the ride. I was involved with a few press interviews, talking as best I could, but struggling considerably given the terrible state of my voice. Confusingly, I wasn't tired. At least, I didn't think I was. I was fatigued, but the euphoria of having finished put me in an overly alert state (so I thought). I was still talking utter nonsense to those around me, but at least I was talking. Episodes of film from after the finish demonstrate my inability to answer questions, but at least I gave the responses I did with enthusiasm.

Standing on the spot where I dismounted the bike for the last time suddenly put me in a position that I hadn't even thought about. There was a crowd of people gathered and staring at me, but I didn't have the faintest idea what to say to them. In the clearest voice I could find I muttered a few words of relief and then thanked them all for coming down and for their invaluable support along the roadside. It was a delight to have so many people present, and so many people who had put in an extraordinary effort to be there. I was very humbled. I feel I did a poor job of chatting to them, so I hope they understood that I just wanted to rest my legs and take the situation in myself. To some degree I felt they were all evaluating me in that moment and I felt a little like an animal at the zoo. It was a shock for me, and I really wish I had been able to watch the finish unfold from outside my body. I craved food and drink, somewhere soft and warm that I might be able to lie down, and a firm, but relaxing massage. I felt pretty terrible actually and had had enough of suffering publicly.

Inevitably, and thankfully not before long, conversations turned to food and we really were in need of nutritional sustenance. A cooked breakfast, my first proper meal post-ride, was suggested and so we took off for Penzance to find the best fry up that money could buy. To be honest, an ice cold bowl of cereal would have gone down a treat, particularly if it was soggy and I hadn't needed to chew it, but a cooked breakfast sounded the next best thing. Fortunately we found the biggest, trucker sized portions that our stomachs were looking for.

While the team devoured their meals, I sat slumped in my chair, dozing at every opportunity. Dressed in the most inappropriate summer clothing, I resembled something from the 1960's, clad in my bright orange 'hippie' jumper, reverse retro cap and baggy grey sweat pants. I awoke to the sight of the entire team and my parents across the table, and smiled at having everyone together in the same place. I felt like I was finally done and I was content with the feeling of satisfaction that the entire project had worked. The team and I had made it, somehow, against all the doubts and the troubles. We'd sorted every problem we encountered on the route and managed to shave 23 hours from the previous record.

However, in the midst of this very happy feeling and to shatter all happy peaceful thoughts I might have just conjured up, I suddenly became acutely aware that I still had little control over my bladder. I had been drinking a lot since I finished in an attempt to soften the desert-like texture in my mouth, so I was sure I would need to release some fluids pretty soon. I made my way over to the public toilets, hobbling and guiding myself with the use of railings and whatever I could get my hands on. I must have looked like a seriously troubled individual to all those people getting off the train that morning. I stumbled through the toilets and towards the empty cubicle at the end of the row. I staggered past a respectable looking man in a suit who looked at me with great disdain, and a hint of disgust at my rather shabby appearance. Had I stopped to explain, my appearance would have become a whole lot worse, I can tell you.

I made it through the push door of the cubicle and then fought for a long time to get out of my clothing. The struggle was made all the more difficult by the lack of control in my hands. They had swollen to such a great size and were void of all feeling that they acted more like clubs than dextrous implements. Finally I was undressed and I fell back onto the loo, glad of somewhere to sit down. It was amazing how much of a struggle this process was. My body knew it had finished the ride. It seemed to go into an immediate recovery mode, making even the most simple task an exhausting process. Just getting undressed made me crave food and a rest!

I was woken sometime later by the sound of my Dad's voice checking I was ok. That alone took me back to my early childhood! He was stood outside the cubicles trying to work out where I was for I'd been in there a long time. I tried to get myself dressed, which was more difficult than ever before, but then the real challenge started. To save him standing there expectantly, I told him I'd be out shortly and to give me a minute. My greatest battle was about to commence; undoing the lock on the door.

Having managed to push the slider across, I lacked the ability to move it back with my fingers. Regretfully (in hindsight), I began thumping the door with my hands and elbows, causing quite a ruckus. Eventually the latch moved causing the door to bend inwards and I was able to slide outside and waddle through the toilets, almost dressed, using the walls as a means of stabilising myself. Still groggy and grumpy from my sleep, and only able to half open my eyes, I was moaning in response to the pain still surging through my body with every step. Every movement, particularly planting my foot, caused me trouble. I couldn't stand up straight or fully extend either leg. My head hung troubled, my chin closely acquainted with my chest and my arms swung aimlessly by my side, ready to lash out and grab something more stable than myself at any moment. My legs were unable to deal with the weight of my body, so I had to continually rock around, trying to share the load across all the joints.

I made it over to the hand washer that was operated by a series of press-buttons. I stood side by side with another suited man who looked at me with even greater disgust. The anger and disappointment on his face would ordinarily have caused me to confront him, but I was too tired and struggling too much to get these buttons pressed. The man in the corner stood back, not getting too close to this terrible looking and smelling human that was stood thumping the buttons of the washer. I was failing to get it to work, and I was certainly getting no help from that man beside me. His main concern was whether he should act on his instinct to call the police and report me for administering serious drugs in the toilets – that was clearly his thought process.

Fortunately my Dad then came back in to make sure I wasn't still asleep. He aided my situation by explaining to the angry looking man that I was not an excessive drug user, but I had in actual fact just been on a bike non-stop for almost six days. Once they had come round to believing his story they changed their attitude toward me; one of them even pressed the washer's buttons for me and was caring enough to make sure the soap landed on my hands. That was a perfect reminder for me not to judge someone by their appearance.

My Dad smiled at their prejudices and then helped me back out to where the rest of the team were loading the vans, ready to return home. What excitement that caused – the thought of getting home. I ambled into the motor home, eyeing up one of the beds that I had been dreaming about through the whole ride. I chatted to Chloe about how I was feeling and she comforted me by telling me that with time she would be able to help put me back together. She was so reassuring and I loved getting to hold her hand and chat about my problems. I was also able to sit with Pete and talk over what had just happened. I was so glad to have shared that experience with Pete – he is a true inspiration and selflessly gave everything he had to make that ride take place.

Just as I sat down on the bed, excited for the impending sleep, a large rush of blood appeared down my body, covering my clothes and the floor. My nose was gushing blood. The team joked that I needed to drain the EPO somewhere, and in the dirty, wrecked van it seemed a perfect place! Of course, they were joking about the EPO. Such things are not for me. Not when Hartley's jelly and Pete's tuna sandwiches are available. Being too impatient to sit and pinch my nose I instead opted to stuff my nostrils with tissue paper and lay back in the bed.

My head seemed to be engulfed by the abundance

of pillows and cushions that had hidden the mattress. My head felt well protected and caressed by something other than the same sweaty helmet that had been clasped around my head for so long. It was wonderful to have a soft material resting against my cheeks and not that salt-caked strap. I will also never forget the truly orgasmic feeling of the duvet as I pulled it up tight to my face and snuggled into with every inch of my body that still had feeling registering the caressing pleasure that the soft sheet provided. I wriggled my legs under the duvet and enjoyed one of those 'morning stretches', which feel full of effort, but barely require any movement at all. What was even more delightful than the duvet or the pillows was accepting the tiredness that I felt, feeling my eyelids battle with the task of remaining open, and then saying to myself: "go ahead, enjoy the sleep. Sleep for however long you wish and when you wake up, you won't have to cycle a bike again".

As I fell into a lovely deep sleep, full of the thoughts of the ride, the blood dried over my face, adding to the unwashed, unchanged and weathered mess that I was now maintaining as my appearance. It was a pathetic attempt at a long sleep. After one hour I awoke rather abruptly. I woke to see the team relaxed and chatting away, but couldn't work out why I was in the van, clearly sleeping, and yet it was moving. It was a surge of fear that something was wrong, and then that beautiful realisation hit me; I was done. I didn't have to cycle anymore. Chloe was the first person to chat to me, setting my mind at ease and reminding me that I was all finished. She set to work checking me over and making sure things were ok. I found myself pouring my heart out to Chloe and discussing even more concerns with her. There were so many issues with my body that I needed to talk about, from swollen and numb hands to missing testicles and a bleeding arse, but nothing fazed her in the slightest. It was a pleasure to have someone with her attitude looking after me. Poor Ben, meanwhile, was still driving the motor home and he was on his own mission to reach his finish line in Taunton. Unbelievably, he had to get back to work!

Once back in Taunton, I was under Chloe orders that someone else had to check me over so she took me to the hospital to try and get some help for the growing problems and injuries that I had accrued over the course of the time on the bike. I stood (I use that loosely) before the front desk at the hospital reception trying to explain coherently what exactly was wrong with me. I started by complaining about being tired; really very tired indeed. Then I described my feet and worked my way up from the floor so as not to forget anything that had gone wrong with my body and mind. I felt bad for the lady, and also everyone else who was in earshot, for not sparing any details about the type of sores I had. The receptionist's mouth opened and the confused frown began to take over her face. She looked mightily unsure if I was making this up. I was still wearing the same ridiculous clothing, had blood dried across my face, and hadn't washed for a week.

She looked back and forth from her computer before telling me that my circumstances didn't fit into one of the 'boxes' on her screen. Looking unsure what to do, she smiled and said "I know, I'll just pop you down as unwell." After a couple of seconds where I processed what she'd just said, I beamed a genuine smile. I was certain that most people in the hospital were unwell, but this was her well-crafted decision about how best to describe my condition. It was a sure fire box to tick though. I was admitted for being unwell. Perfect.

The doctor who came to see me clearly didn't believe the story that I was telling him. I had to have it verified by Chloe who was also in the cubicle with me, otherwise I think I would have been washed and sent through to a psychiatric unit. Thankfully he came around to the idea that I really had been stuck on a bike and he attended to more of my worries. He was highly reluctant (who can blame him) to view my arse, instead preferring to base his opinions on my descriptions alone. I hope I am not being too offensive in describing some of my issues, but once I'd told him I had lost my testicles inside me he decided that he'd better take a look. His observation from the imprints in my skin that I rode a Fizik saddle was something I found interesting, but more than my interest, it highlighted that my bottom half had taken a real battering. He seemed unconcerned about the lack of feeling in my lower back and thighs, suggesting it would all return in due course. Although I wasn't happy with that response at the time, doctors are usually right. And he was.

They performed several blood tests to make sure things were ok internally, with the results highlighting a high level of protein in the blood. This didn't surprise me at all, but the doctors wanted to ensure my kidneys were functioning sufficiently. Plenty of food and fluids and ample rest were the prescriptions I was given, and I had to make sure I headed back for more tests once I had rested (and was starting to make more sense). I was relying too much on Chloe to comprehend everything that was going on, but she was aware that I was slow at processing and explained all the information succinctly and clearly for me. My body was so swollen that there was very little the doctors could do for me at that particular time, so after a short while I was sent to the comfort of my home.

Following that trip to the hospital I returned to my parent's house to wash and clean myself up for the first time in almost a week. Getting up the stairs, out of my clothes and into the shower required some significant assistance. But the struggle up the stairs was worth it. I enjoyed the feeling of the warm water, pounding against my skin and washing away the stress of the previous six days. It was all over and my worries, pains and fears were being washed away. The heat of the shower made my skin tingle, but I at least felt fresh and alive.

Drying myself was a tender and delicate

performance, leading to my decision to abandon the process half way through. I left the bathroom feeling more alive and slightly human again. It was a huge relief to be clean, and with the towel I could feel myself scraping away more of the grime and dirt that had accumulated in, on and around my body during the time on the bike. Now all I wanted was food. But first I needed to get down the stairs. I achieved this faster than hoped. I stood at the top of the stairs and my knees buckled and down I fell. The shock, and the pain in my knees, caused me to yelp (a manly way of screaming?) and I just cried in a sorry heap where I came to a stop. My mother came and sat beside me and I recall longing for the pain to ease. What was going on? I couldn't even stand up by myself. I knew this was going to be a long road to recovery.

It is a road that I am still travelling as I write this, four months after finishing. I am typing this with numb hands, the result of nerve damage caused by compression and vibration. The balls of my feet and my toes are also without feeling, leaving me with awkward moments when walking upstairs, but otherwise useful for wearing shoes that are too small. I still suffer the effects of extreme tiredness and I find myself sleeping far more than I ever did before. My metabolism seems unhappy with me, too. I still crave huge amounts of food and although I try to limit my calorie intake now I am not exercising to the same extreme, I often struggle to satisfy my constant urge to eat. I have attempted to exercise a little over the course of the four months, but I fall prey to an overwhelming urge to stop. My body instantly feels tired and weak and craves rest. Even the most gentle exercise feels as though it might induce a significant bonk. I struggle to sit on a hard chair for more than ten minutes before the pain throughout my rear end becomes excruciating. The bruising from my fractured bones took over a month to surface, leaving me still with black toes, but fortunately I have limited feeling in these. My main priority now is getting feeling back in my hands.

**

Completing this ride is perhaps one of the most challenging tasks I have ever set myself. I hope I never forget the moment that I finished the ride, for it was the culmination of months and months of hard work and determination (from many people). That finish line, for me, was the end of an 18 month cycling adventure, not just the event's six days. Not only was I getting off the bike that morning, but also I was getting off the bike on which I had been living for over a year. I was returning to a life that had been all but consumed by two wheels and I longed for a morning where I could roll over in bed for an extra hour's sleep; for an afternoon where I could simply sit in a field with a good book. I wanted my life back.

Training for this ride and then the ride itself had been a completely life changing experience. I had had to adjust almost every aspect of my day-to-day life, altering my work commitments, my research commitments and my social commitments. I became a relative loner, save my companionship in the wheels. I learned more than I ever thought I could about the South West's roads and I have eaten more calories than I would like to recall. Over the course of the training period I consumed an average of 8000 calories per day, over three times the recommended intake for an adult male. It has been calculated that during the event itself I was burning almost 20 000 calories per 24 hours. That equates to 50 mars bars each day. Since returning to normal life I have clung to the remains of that full time cycling diet – the one thing I no longer needed in my suddenly sedentary life.

I have grown fat and lazy. I now sit behind a computer most of the day reading and writing for my PhD. It has been a complete change from all things physical to all things mental. I haven't made the transition very effectively, maintaining my obsessive compulsion to stick with a task until completion. However I find it much more challenging to sit behind a computer, motionless, having spent so long in search of the best down hills to ride as fast as I can. I miss that relationship I had with cycling, but I know I have to rest and afford my body time to recover before I start preparing for the next challenge.

I have been delighted and, on occasions, moved to tears by some of the stories I've heard since being back from the ride. I have had hundreds of people contact me to tell me of their own personal challenges they've been inspired to complete since following / hearing about my venture. I have found this truly humbling and it is exactly what I had hoped to result from this ride. I have been fortunate and honoured to offer advice to many people planning their future ventures, and have been over the moon to receive offers to partake in many inspiring upcoming events.

However, I have left my body with several issues that it needs to repair. As I have described, I finished the ride with those multiple injuries, many of which will require ongoing treatment. Although in these four months the majority of the injuries have healed, my hands remain clumsy and awkward. I look forward to the day when I might, once again, be able to dress myself with ease, or turn the pages of a book one at a time.

I think the biggest thank you I need to offer is to each and every member of the support team. Without their unfaltering efforts and enthusiasm I would certainly have failed this task. This ride was such a tremendous team effort. Had there been any difference in the team members then it would have been such a different story. They allowed me to come up with this ludicrous idea and then they nurtured the ideas and supported me from the very first moment until we crossed the finish line. During the ride they were pushed outside their comfort zones, working in conditions that were far from comfortable. They had to contend with all manner of things of which I am not placed to comment. I have no idea what they would have gone through during those six days. I can only speculate, and in attempting to do so, I would make some very big errors. For that reason I have included at the end here, some of their accounts of the ride and their experiences throughout.

I chose the team members each for very specific reasons, but also because I knew each of them would bring something unique to the team environment. It was one of the most difficult decisions to make during the entire process, but I made eight decisions that I was extremely pleased with. I won't ever be able to show them enough gratitude for the time and efforts they sacrificed in helping me achieve this ambition.

I guess that's where I draw the curtains on recounting my experience of LEJOGLE and that particular relationship with cycling. Writing about it has almost followed a similar pattern of events. At the beginning I was totally unsure whether it was a sensible idea or whether I had a hope of completing it. I dived in and there was an initial period where I was making fantastic progress and eagerly hoping the impressive advancement would continue. Then the dreaded emotional undulations that threaten to send the original idea and all its glory to an early grave, yet offer just enough hope to save it from an anti-climatic failure, before finally receiving a few heartbeats of encouragement that would carry me, somewhat unaware of the world around me, toward a long awaited finish line.

Amongst my ramblings about this rather significant event in my life, I hope I have managed to convey those three critical features that I consider essential for personal achievement: Creative thought, Self-Belief and Determination. If this account has encouraged you to better yourself on a bike then I am flattered by the impact of my ride. If it has impacted upon you to change your life in any capacity, even the way you approach the idea of what you consider possible, then I am truly honoured and I thank you for your time. I hope we can all make a huge difference and learn that we really can astound ourselves.

After word: Andy Shaw of the Links Risk Advisory.

"If you are going to win any battle, you have to do one thing.
You have to make the mind run the body." (G.S. Patton).

Mental arithmetic is my thing; I could never really spell. I find counting numbers quickly and calculating odds, darts scores, or restaurant bills a skill that comes to me naturally. So when the barman at my local pub calmly stated he was intending to cycle from Land's End to John O'Groats and back again in a record time of six days, it didn't take more than the time it took him to pour me a pint of beer to realise he was either a phenomena, or simply a deranged dreamer. Regardless of which he was, I thought, he's in for an enormous helping of pain and discomfort.

There's something about Ben Rockett that you can't forget. While his affable nature immediately puts people at ease, a quality that makes him a great barman, and his sandy hair suggests his rightful place is flexing his torso as a lifeguard on a sunny Cornish beach, there's a unique determination in his eyes when he's talking about taking on a challenge that captivates people. It makes them sit up and take notice. I didn't get involved in supporting Ben for any other reason than I love someone not just with the passion to dream, and indeed to dream big, but also with the intent to take their challenge head on and to go out and achieve. The World needs more people like Ben, and to say he took his challenge head on is an understatement. Regardless of the questions his epic journey asked of him, he had the answers, and he delivered those answers with some style. I have been lucky enough to work with a number of Gold medal winning Olympic athletes during my career and it struck me as we went through the initial planning phases with Ben that he made the other elite athletes I know look lazy. And I don't imagine there are many Olympians who struggle to get an hour's sleep a night for six days in the pursuit of their medal.

I'm humbled to have been given a chance to support something so uplifting. I feel lucky to have had an inside view of everything that happened. I'm excited to see what the guy does next. I hope my 2 year old daughter grows up to follow his example.

Andy Shaw
Links Risk Advisory

*"Friendship, like phosphorous, shines brightest when all around
is dark."*

(Proverb).

Alastair Steel:

I met Alastair through the Pulteney Arms in Bath. He was a regular face across the bar and soon became interested in the ride following my search for a website builder. As the months passed I managed to twist his arm into lending his office in central Bath to become the 'Rockettrides HQ' where we would hold team meetings, have route planning sessions, store all the equipment and supplies, and work the phones in search of sponsors and publicity. By the time August came around, Alastair was confirmed as one of the drivers for the support vehicles.

During the course of the ride however, Alastair fulfilled numerous roles within the team; from driving, to organising people and 'overseeing' what everyone was up to. His often selfless behaviour summarised his dedication to making this event a success and I believe he felt a tremendous pressure to ensure the safety of everyone involved. Throughout the preparation stages he was easily the most involved logistically. Not once did he join me on the bike, but I put that down to him being caught up organising and planning for what seemed like every eventuality. I didn't actually see him very much over those 1900 miles. I took this to mean he was busy. I will always be grateful for the commitment he showed towards this silly idea, the hours and hours of stressful planning that have contributed toward the ebbing of his hair and the efforts he made chasing sponsors and such like. I am still quite unsure how to go about saying a good enough thank you.

Some of his own memories include: "During the first night and following ridiculous rain, Ben was already missing the services of a proper physio. Everyone made their best efforts which were appreciated however, but I turned my attention to the police car that had been tipped off that there were some people doing despicable things to a poor man in a lay-by. I went for a chat with the policeman, vaguely conscious that my hair was all over the place, I had food stains down the front of my shirt and was beginning to smell. This didn't seem to detract from my explanation and the policeman wished us well and drove off.

As we followed Ben, there were two things occupying most of my mind apart from driving or navigating. How do we make the stops flow more easily and aren't we going a bit fast? I had earlier managed to check that our GPS position was finding its way onto Ben's website. Reading some of the messages was when I realised that reading words of support was something I would have to avoid. They were causing me to get rather large lumps in my throat.

Several hundred miles further South we stopped for food. I was expecting Ben to be in a bad way when he arrived but it was worse than ever. It was clearly a struggle for Ben to control the bike as he turned into the car park and the others rushed to help him off. Ben came into the motor home and we went to the rear of the van. He looked at me, cried and said he didn't think he could make it.

Ben Allen:

Ben and I met back in a geography class at Richard Huish College. We soon established a whole host of mutual interests and found ourselves attending Wurzel concerts (no, I am still not ashamed of that yet), going on long 'adventure walks' and generally being outside getting up to mischief. Over the years Ben has become a very close friend indeed and I was eager to get him into the support crew as soon as possible. He is one of the most laid back and thoughtful people I have ever had the pleasure to know and I consider him an invaluable asset to the whole team. Ben was appointed 'vehicle manager' and was set to undertake a big share of the support vehicle driving. He did far more than his fair share.

During those long miles on the bike, Ben was the most comforting team member. He offered me calming, supportive, honest updates and when I was at my most broken and upset he was always there with a warming cuddle. I felt comforted by his presence and knew he was working his heart out to complete his job, and anything else which needed doing far beyond that which he was expected. Being such a gentle, caring giant of a man, I believe Ben was an aid to everyone in that supporting vehicle, not just me out on that bike. His partner, Lucy, once said to me "my Ben will do anything for anyone and that's why I love him". He truly would. What a team player.

Ben's account remembers: "The next stop was in the Midlands. After we man-handled Ben and forced him to eat, we set off and were soon averaging an incredible speed of 28mph. Although I was worried this speed would burn Ben out, at the same time it would put in some cushion time for any problems later on. Also there was the issue that if he didn't beat the record significantly I would be late for work on the Friday afternoon so part of me thought this would save me a bollocking!! At this point Ben was still looking strong and although he had made small moans and groans and the weather was really wet and windy, it didn't seem like there was any major issues to worry about.

In Scotland we followed the road for what seemed like an age and although it was dark you could tell the mountains were massive. There were deer on the roads and it was here, a short distance from Fort William that Ben had his first sleep on the bike. I was map reading and Dan driving, we said we could see him dozing off and then his head dropped and his hands went limp on the bars, his legs span slower and slower before he was just coasting along. Dan sounded the horn and for the first few blasts there was no effect but then Ben woke up and just looked down at the bike and continued to cycle. The whole incident only lasted 20 seconds or so but it is something I will never forget especially with the surroundings. These roads were a blessing as there was no other traffic around and at about 6am we stopped alongside the loch. The mosquitoes were incredible, so were the views. It struck me how ugly the houses around this lovely loch were.

When Ben arrived at JOG he stopped the bike, got off and just fell into my arms; he was in a real state. We embraced for a while; it wasn't a cuddle or a hug it was more than that - he had got this far but now felt terrible in every way. The physical pain was obvious. If you try to cycle that distance that quickly, in bad weather with no sleep it is bound to be nasty. I knew I would see Ben at his lowest and all I could do was offer him a massive embrace, which seemed to last ages. Following this Ben got in the camper and had some food. In the light of the camper he looked even more ruined and complained a lot about the weather.

The vehicle was in a real state. Not only was there the smell that only lots of sleeping men can make, there was the stale sweat of the outriders' and Ben's cycle clothing being dried out on the air blowers that added a rare smell, too. But all these fragrances were trumped by the distinctly strong smell of urine. In my cab at the front of the camper I didn't smell it too badly unless I braked hard and it rolled along the under floor to the front and this even caused urine to appear in the foot wells!

Chloe Felton:

I met Chloe while we were on the running team together at college, and although the only times I was able to chat to her were before we started and quite some time after we'd finished, there was something about her I admired. Chloe had a very caring nature and a great sense of humour; not to mention tenacity and grit. Following our college days, Chloe went on to study Physiotherapy, and during those years at University, we would often discuss training and races. I always trusted Chloe and knew that her healing hands would be capable of mending almost any troubles. I asked Chloe to come along on the ride and help me with physio treatments as and when they were required. I was delighted when she accepted.

You can imagine my concern when I found out she was very unwell and unable to make the start of the ride. I was concerned for her health and selfishly concerned for the ride. I'd imagined Chloe to be my main emotional support on the road. I often thought about her in those first few days, wondering how she was feeling and what she would make of the Heath Robinson attempts of massage and physio from the others. I liked to picture her laughing at us all.

There are a few feelings and experiences I will never forget from the ride, but one of the most uplifting moments was reaching through the window and having

Chloe hold my hand. What a delight and utter relief it was to see her there. Her smile alone soothed the pains and looking at her I knew we would make it to the end. Chloe is one amazingly special person and I was honoured to have her join us for the final stages. Thank you Chloe for the immense effort you made to be with us.

Dan Tudge:

It was my pleasure to be introduced to Dan Tudge one weekend a few years back while he was home from his RAF duties. He was a very keen triathlete having recently competed in Ironman Switzerland. There is something about Dan's character which comes through immediately. Regardless of the company, Dan is the same person and this consistency of character was something I massively respected. I met with Dan more often and soon we were in regular contact. Dan was present when I first thought about putting the support crew together and he declared his interest to be involved straight away. I was very happy to have him on board and knew that he would play a pivotal role in the whole venture. Dan was a support rider, motivator and driver. It is fair to say that he held the voice of reason and was the main person in making me see sense. I respect him very highly for every aspect of who he is.

Dan's memories include: "It was climb after climb and the Rockett was already fatigued. I spoke to Will at one point about how Ben was struggling at times and explained that I was concerned about how early on in the ride this was happening. Will's response was "Yeh he's fucked, but the thing is, he rides fucked at 20mph". What Will had said was dead right. He was struggling, there was no doubt about it, and at times he was seriously in trouble. But he always pushed on and managed to collect himself.

Another point that was particularly concerning about the ride was when Ben went mad. I had been cycling beside him and chatting about all sorts on the way down through Glasgow. He seemed to be in great spirits. But it soon became clear that, although he had energy and was pedalling, he was mentally tired. He asked me whether I remembered being there before. I replied "yes, on the way up!" He said "no, when we were younger – don't you remember?" I replied "Err, remember what?" - I had genuinely been taken by surprise – one minute we were talking, the next he was going on about random crap. He kept on about how he recognised all the traffic lights and man holes etc etc. I got on the radio and we pulled him into the motor home for a chat and some amateur assessment.

The last 50 miles were great. Ben was in a bad way, of course, but I think anyone who had seen his "really really bad" knew that he had this in the bag. The final leg was immense. The last 10 miles increased in pace from a casual spin to a flat out time trial! I think we had all forgotten about the hills. Grossly underestimating the terrain and distance, we all raced to the line, literally on the rivet. An amazing moment.

Pete Scull:

I met Pete through the Coach Education programme at Bath University. Pete and I always had something to discuss as more often than not he or I would be undertaking some kind of challenge or have an entry to a competition. If neither happened to be doing anything, we would chat about future plans and what crazy ideas we'd heard other people undertaking. Pete had just graduated from the programme and was about to embark on his own gruelling ultra-distance running event. When he expressed a desire to do something with his summer, I was eager to invite him into the team. I had barely finished my sentence before he had agreed. Pete played a truly critical role in the team. He was a chief navigator, chef, kit supplier, data collector, he handled all the calls and emails from supporters and media; his job was holding everything together!

I guess in writing this book I get to have the printed version of what people did within the team! Pete was a key player in making things happen. He put everyone and everything before himself and all the team members have commented on how he slaved away to get things done for others. I doubt the team would have operated so efficiently without him there. My major memories of Pete were as he'd slide under the massage table and read me messages of support. Or how he conveyed the entertaining conversations he was having with friends back home. I appreciated his impeccable timing and endless energies whenever I saw him.

Pete's recollections go something like this: I was drunk when Ben first spoke to me about his plans for the summer of 2010. I hadn't expected him to take me up on my offer to help out with the ride, but looking back, one of the most enjoyable aspects of the ride was having the responsibility of Ben's phone. Messages were regularly coming in and whether it would be out of the window or when we stopped I would read messages to Ben that I thought were going to benefit his morale. The texts were wonderful; encouragement, jokes, quotes, stories and just general well wishes for Ben.

I remember when he was really broken and he looked completely empty. He would always be asking for one of my tuna sandwiches and I made sure there was always food available for him as well as everyone else in the team. Not being able to drive the vehicles meant I was determined to ensure I would do everything else that I could to help the team out. I am not sure whether Ben was just being polite, because he must have been so bored of chicken wraps and tuna sandwiches that week, but he put up with all the food I prepared for him.

One thing I endeavour to forget happened with only a few miles to go. It suddenly occurred to me that after 6 days on the road I had grown a scruffy and unfortunate looking moustache. Realising I had no shaving foam but with a desperation to shave I turned to sun cream. Shaving in a moving motor home, with only sun cream and bottled water actually worked rather well. Pleased with my success I settled in for the last miles of the ride.

Tom Emery:

Tom's role in the challenge was that of camera man and support vehicle driver. His nature is such that Tom brings a smile through a quirky comment at even the most difficult of times. I met Tom through the University of Bath volleyball team and we've developed a close friendship over the last five years. As a lover of the great outdoors and as someone who is keen to be active all the time, Tom is someone who is a pleasure to be around. With a strong caring nature and a wonderful sense of humour, I requested Tom joined the team and bring his guitar to boost morale.

Of all the people in the team I remember being able to communicate with Tom with nothing more than our eyes. Sometimes we'd glare, widen our eyelids, crumple them with pain, roll them with despair or wink them with enjoyment. We didn't need to pass many words to get our thoughts across. I turned to Tom for advice and support. Having had my first stern telling off from Tom during my training I knew he was honest and to the point. That was essential. As one of the smartest individuals I know, I believe Tom found it hard being cooped in a small van, doing nothing but stare at me for six days. He still came through – what a legend.

Tom recalls some entertaining memories: I managed to grab an excellent spot for my bag, under the seats of the van. This backfired after day four when we discovered the van's toilet was leaking, and my bag became drenched in our own urine. Tasty.

I remember Will and Dan coming in off their bikes, both buzzing from a good ride in the sun, and laughing and joking. I snapped. I could have throttled either one of them, what gave them the right to be so happy? Sat on their bloody bikes, enjoying the sun, getting exercise. Bastards! I ridiculously became really stressed with Dan and Will, they were really happy and talking about riding. I was finding it hard being so inactive for so long.

I remember hating the feeling of seeing someone who I've always known to be a very positive and happy person completely broken, angry, tired and in a lot of pain. And from the van that is all I saw. I think this added to my frustrations. I can vividly remember Ben saying everything he wanted to say with just a few moments of eye contact. Whether this was before a big hug or as he wept away, he seemed to convey everything he needed to with just his eyes. Of course I could tell he was in pain from the rest of his body parts that were dragging along the ground behind him!

We shot on ahead to get into Land's End before the riders. I think all the non-riding team were envious of the finish, to have been in the group that cycled over the line with Ben would have been incredible, not so people would have seen us do it, but to have finished as a team behind Ben riding over the line to finish what was an epic challenge and adventure.

Tony Solon:

When I moved back to Bath I did so with a greater involvement in cycling. I soon bumped into Tony on the road bikes and together we spun many routes around Bath and the surrounding area. His attempts to get me into mountain biking, his first love, failed badly but we continued to ride big and regular miles on the thinner tyres. Spending time with Tony was easy and his enthusiasm and interest in cycling is hard to rival. We'd shared many dinners together, spent hours racing on the computer and talked until the cows came home about cycle events and challenges. I asked Tony to come along as support vehicle driver and support rider.

During the ride itself, the relationship between Tony and I evolved somewhat. Tony was to ride with me at my most extreme ends of the tiredness and lucidity scales making his role extremely complicated. I relied on Tony to be a hard task master, then became grumpy with him when he set those tasks! I didn't make his life easy. I most fondly remember night riding with Tony and chatting about utter rubbish. I am sure he will recall more than I can, but I hold Tony responsible for ironing out my mental 'craziness'. He put up with my anger, my wailing, kept all sorts of problems away from me so I could continue riding, and took great concern over my health. I am extremely lucky to have met Tony prior to this venture.

Tony's memories include: "Ben clearly had his mind set on some big miles in the first 24 hours. That's one of the things I realised about Ben whilst getting to know him during training for the event. He might say something along the lines of "I'm going to push for 350 plus miles in the first 24 hours" – what this means in Ben code is – "I won't settle for anything less than 400" – but being as modest as he is you won't learn of his plan to over-achieve until it inevitably comes to fruition! Sure enough he managed a ridiculous 420miles in the first 24 hours. At the time I was a little nervous that he might be sprinting out of the gates too fast – but I also knew he was eager to set his mark on the LEJOGLE record very early in the ride – so I wasn't that surprised.

Tiredness at this point was becoming a problem. Additionally he was starting to constantly complain about foot discomfort. I put this down to the fact that it had been lashing rain all evening and that his feet were presumably soaking wet. However I was to learn much later that these were the first symptoms of his broken foot. But like Ben tends to do in his modest manner, he mentioned the discomfort a few times and then proceeded to just absorb the pain within himself - not mentioning it again until near the end of the ride. He has a crazily powerful mindset when he wants it.

By Glasgow going south, Ben was at a completely different level of exhaustion – something I had never witnessed before. I immediately realised it was going to be a major struggle to keep him awake. I tried all of the tricks I had up my sleeve to keep him alert. We cycled along singing Bon Jovi tunes and trying to remember the lyrics to others for a couple of hours. We had a few enjoyable conversations about star constellations and the Universe. However he started to verbally ramble quite a bit suggesting that we were cycling in circles and that we had already cycled down the roads we were on. I thought he was astutely realising that we were cycling South on the same road on which we cycled North, but in fact he continuously believed that we were cycling repetitively on the same sections of road again and again. I wasn't sure how to deal with this.

As we exited Penzance the sun had just started to rise and we were all of a sudden out of the saddle sprinting like men possessed. When I had a slight chance I remember seeing 30mph on my cyclometer – I simply couldn't believe Ben was able to hold that pace after riding 1800+ miles. I glanced at him from time to time on that final section and saw a seriously grimaced face clearly in agony. I could also see a week's worth of emotions starting to come out which drove us all on to keep his pace as high as possible for the final few miles. The extent of the adrenaline rush was something I had never experienced before, which is probably why we were able to hold an average of 30 mph for the last 10 miles! As we neared the very end, Ben insisted that we remain beside him. I really hadn't expected to be given the great honour of accompanying him across the finish line and was overwhelmed to do so.

William Collins:

Will Collins was my first thought for a team member when I started planning the whole challenge. Will and I met through college and I was instantly amazed by his enjoyment of a challenge. He was a super keen triathlete who loved competing. Will has one of the best personalities I know. He would definitely be described as the joker and no situation can be truly terrible while he is around. At times when there seems no answer, Will pipes up with his response, guaranteed. As an extremely capable cyclist and with a sound mechanical knowledge, Will was the first person I asked to be a member of the team. Owing to his work commitments in France it became a challenge to set the ride's start date, but I was prepared to adjust this as necessary in order to have him along.

Over the course of the end to end to end, Will was just as I thought Will would be. He lightened the mood, he was supportive, abusive, entertaining, full of endless chatter, and the phenomenal friend that I had come to know. He allowed me to be ruthlessly rude to him, to scream tears of pain at him and to be so mean that most people would have taken serious offence. As it happened, Will laughed at me and encouraged me some more. When I asked for some of his memories he produced the following:

Pre-LEJOGLE I did not have much to do with it as handily I was working abroad. I returned to what can only be described as a pretty serious operation with an HQ, maps, sponsors and the like. I was pretty impressed with what Ben had achieved, and it was excellent to know it was going ahead.

For the ride it was the worst weather I have ever seen for an entire week and this meant Ben had to ride through constant rain. I am not even being dramatic about this; it was horrendous the whole time. The week after it was beautiful which made me laugh.

The first night I rode with Ben, the only way I can describe him is as a total asshole! He basically made me ride with him for 8 hours without talking. Every time I turned to check how he was doing, all I saw was this downtrodden, beaten face and I seriously thought he was not going to make it. He needed a serious kick up the arse and I basically said 'stop being a total fool, you decided to do this'. Now, he has probably not printed what I actually wrote but you can get the gist. After that he stopped being grumpy.

We made it to Scotland without too much of a problem, but you cannot understand how bloody long Scotland is. You could easily cut half of Scotland away and it would still be too big. And it would make LEJOGLE much easier. The only good thing about it is the mountains, for they are awesome!

Ben really slowed in that section and I rode with him to Wick. I remember him asking me how far it was. I loved that road; it was brilliant - sharp sweeping descents and killer climbs – Ben hated it understandably as he had been on the bike for nearly 2 days! I just said to Ben 'only about 8 miles now' not having a bloody clue where we actually were. We turned the next bend and a massive road sign said Wick 25 miles. It was torture but I found it secretly funny. Also, all we wanted was a McDonalds. I was riding with Ben a lot, and on its own I was doing big mileage but comparing it to Ben, 6,7,8,9,10 even 11 hours was nothing. It went from being a physical test to a mental ordeal right there. We were not yet half way. Then I thought 'this guy is stupid. He is already broken and he still has to ride back.'